The Trainee Teachers' Survival Guide
(Second edition)

D1255356

Also available from Continuum:

How to Survive Your First Year in Teaching 2nd edition, Sue Cowley

Everything You Need to Know to Survive Teaching 2nd edition, The Ranting Teacher

Taking the Stress Out of Bad Behaviour: Behaviour Management of 3–11 year olds, Simon Brownhill

Getting the Buggers to Behave 3rd edition, Sue Cowley

100 Ideas for Trainee Teachers, Angella Cooze

So You Want to be a Teacher? Lucy Waide

The Trainee Teachers' Survival Guide

(Second edition)

HAZEL BENNETT

continuum

Continuum International Publishing Group

The Tower Building   80 Maiden Lane, Suite 704
11 York Road   New York,
SE1 7NX   NY 10038

www.continuumbooks.com

British Library Cataloguing-in-Publication Data
A catalogue record for this book is available from the British Library.

ISBN: 9781847060563 (paperback)

Library of Congress Cataloging-in-Publication Data
A catalog record for this book is available from the Library of Congress.

Typeset by BookEns Ltd, Royston, Hertfordshire
Printed and bound in Great Britain by Antony Rowe, Chippenham, Wilts.

To Graham, Russell, Alicia and Michael

Contents

Acknowledgements

I should like to thank the following teachers for their help in compiling this book:

Katrina Beciri
Russell Bennett
Steve Bloom
Carole Edwards
Adam Haffner
Shirin Haidari
Claire Hart
Emma Laikin
Sorana Leach
Cecilia McKeague
Helen Pallet
Kevin Paradise
Philip Rosenthal
Elaine Wilson

With special thanks to Kate Nivison for her expert guidance.

1 | Preparation for training

Why be a teacher?

The teaching profession offers the opportunity to make a major contribution to the quality of life of the nation's children – in fact, its future. Grateful pupils remember competent teachers for the rest of their lives, and the job offers levels of satisfaction and pleasure that, for many teachers, outweigh having to accept a lower salary than those in some other professions.

But do note: choosing the right career for you is very important, because the wrong choice can result in a loss of precious time and energy.

In the past the cynical saying, 'Those who can, do. Those who can't, teach', did have a grain of truth in it as some people only went into teaching after being turned down by their first choice of career. Some people drift into teaching, after university in particular, because they are not sure what to do with their working life.

The course is intensive and time-consuming, and so it is important not to enter it unless you are absolutely certain that teaching is your chosen career.

I have been told by a few students that for them the generous training salary for graduates was a deciding factor. I am, of course, in favour of paying graduates a training salary, because the profession needs new blood and the thought of chalking up another year's worth of debt, without a reasonably high initial salary to make it worthwhile, may deter potential teachers. However, the training salary alone is not an adequate reason to choose teaching.

If you believe anything you have heard about teaching being a nice, comfortable little job – short hours, long holidays – forget it. The contact hours (that is, time actually spent with pupils) can be shorter than those for most jobs – about 28 hours per week – but they can be intensely pressurized. There are also hours of preparation, many hours of marking, record keeping, report writing, looking for lost coats or PE kits, as well as reassuring anxious parents, after-school clubs, open evenings, staff meetings and school journeys.

If you think the holidays are a compensation for the above, you may well find that it sometimes takes a chunk of the holidays to unwind. Moreover, you may not have enough money to go anywhere interesting in comfort for a few years, unless your partner or parents are prepared to subsidize it.

Women may find that people who have never taught will tell them, 'it's a good job for a woman'. By this they mean that you can leave work at 4pm, pick up your own children and have plenty of time to put the dinner on the table for your husband, who has 'done a day's work'. That's nonsense, of course. It's difficult to leave at 4pm because of all the extra tasks and meetings to attend.

Another consideration might be that if you have children of your own, you may feel that you can never escape from children. Unless you have a bottomless pit of patience, you might suffer higher stress levels than childless teachers, or parents who can escape from their children by working with adults. Sometimes you will only be able to cope by arriving at school early, around 7.30am, working through breaks and lunch hours, and taking work home, where it might be difficult to do it because you are beset by demands from your own children.

Teachers themselves sometimes advise their children not to become teachers, although I notice that the advice is rarely accepted. Nevertheless, if you are energetic and creative, enjoy a challenge, are competent at communicating ideas enthusiastically and have a talent for forming easy relationships with a wide range of people, read on. Teaching could well be the perfect job for you.

Choosing the right course

There are now more channels into teaching than ever before.

Undergraduate teacher training
You can train to be a teacher while doing a degree:

◆ *Bachelor of Education Degree course (B.Ed.)*, which gives you four years of teacher training and a qualification that carries Qualified Teacher Status (QTS)
◆ *Bachelor of Arts or Science with QTS.*

Postgraduate teacher training courses – if you already have a degree

◆ *Postgraduate Certificate in Education (PGCE)*. Students are normally based at a college or university for an academic year, and also spend time in schools on teaching practice.

◆ *School Centred Initial Teacher Training (SCITT)*. SCITT courses are organized by local education authorities (LEAs) in England and can also run for an academic year.

Employment-based teacher training

Students train and qualify while working as a teacher.

◆ *Graduate Teacher Programme (GTP)*. A student on a GTP is based in a school for a year as an unqualified employee.

◆ *Registered Teacher Programme (RTP)*. This is for students who have some unqualified teaching experience and the equivalent of two years of higher education.

◆ *Teach First*. This is a two-year course for high-flying graduates to work in a challenging secondary school in Greater London, Greater Manchester and the Midlands.

Qualifications and entrance

At the time of writing (2008), to get onto most teacher training courses you need to have attained a standard of at least a grade C in GCSE English and Maths, and the equivalent of a C in GCSE Science if you want to teach at Key Stage 2 or 3.

For an undergraduate course you will need at least two A levels. You need to contact individual colleges and universities for more details. You normally apply through the Universities and Colleges Admissions Service (UCAS).

For a PGCE, SCITT or GTP course, you also need a UK degree or equivalent. If you are uncertain whether your qualifications are acceptable, you can find out through the UK National Academic Recognition Centre (NARIC; www.naric.org.uk). Your degree should be linked to the subject(s) you want to teach. The SCITT courses are only based in England. Some SCITT courses can award a PGCE qualification.

To apply for a PGCE or SCITT course in most colleges and universities or LEAs, you need to apply to the through the Graduate Teacher Training Registry (www.gttr.ac.uk; phone 0871 468 0469), but check first on each training provider's website because some want you to apply directly to them. You can also get more information from www.tda.gov.uk/Recruit/thetrainingprocess/typesofcourse/scitt.aspx.

You can do the Graduate Teacher Programme in any maintained school in England or Wales if they are prepared to employ you as an unqualified teacher for the year. Independent schools also train GTP students but the school has to fund the course itself. You can find a post by answering an advertisement or applying to the local Employment Based Initial Teacher Training (EBITT) provider (www.tda.gov.uk/partners/recruiting/ebr/drbs/ebittcontacts.aspx). You can also get more information by emailing grtp@tdainfo.co.uk.

The RTP is suitable for people who want to combine work and study. You need to have completed either an HND, a Dip. H.E. or two years of a degree course and you also need to be working in a school as an unqualified teacher. If you apply, you have to find a school that is willing to employ you and help to train you, and then you must apply to your local EBITT, which will assess your application and decide how much further teacher training you need.

Teach First

The two-year Teach First course is run by an independent organization in London, Manchester and the Midlands to train graduates in challenging secondary schools in teaching and leadership skills. The schools work in partnership with businesses. As already mentioned, the course is designed to attract high-flying graduates who wish to pursue a career in teaching, and it gives the opportunity to develop a career in commerce.

Applicants need a 2:1 degree, three Bs at A level and grade C in GCSE Maths and English. They also have to be able to show high levels of the relevant personal attributes such as leadership, teamwork, resilience, critical thinking and the ability to work respectfully and cooperatively with others. All applications are made online through http://teachfirst.org.uk. Teach First accepts applications twice a year, in December and June.

Financial help available for the student teacher

At the time of writing, all students on a full-time teacher training course are eligible for some form of financial help, whether they are on the undergraduate or the postgraduate course.

If your university charges fees, you can apply to your LEA for a loan to pay them. For living costs, students may qualify for a means-tested maintenance grant, which does not need to be repaid. Students normally need to apply for their grant in late February to early March of the year in which they hope to start their course. It is a wise precaution to telephone your LEA early on in the academic year to get the full facts, as they change from year to year.

When sending off an application form as vital as this, it is a sensible precaution to enclose a stamped postcard addressed to yourself with the words 'Application for university fees' written on the back. If you slip in a note asking them to sign the postcard and return it, you can be absolutely certain your application has arrived, which gives you peace of mind from knowing it has not been lost in the post.

Students can apply for a further loan from the Student Loan Company (www.slc.co.uk). This does not need to be paid back until they start earning. The interest rate at the time of writing is 4.8% per annum.

For up-to-date details of other grants and loans, go to www.direct.gov.uk/en/EducationAndLearning/UniversityAndHigherEducation/StudentFinance/FinanceForNewStudents. You can get a DVD to give you full details and you can apply online for loans and grants.

Students from Northern Ireland should apply to the Student Finance NI at www.studentfinanceni.co.uk.

Students from Scotland should apply to the Students Awards Agency for Scotland at www.saas.gov.uk.

Students from Wales should apply to Student Finance Wales at www.studentfinancewales.co.uk.

At the time of writing, students on some PGCE courses are eligible for a 'golden hello' award of up to £5,000 when they have successfully completed their induction year, depending on their subject. 'Golden hellos' are not awarded to SCITT teachers.

Again at the time of writing, eligible students on the PGCE course receive to a tax-free training salary, depending on their subject and course. Other bursaries are available in Wales, but you need to obtain up-to-date information from the appropriate website above.

Trainees on the GTP and RTP courses in England and Wales are paid as unqualified teachers. Currently the rate of pay is about £15,113 (£19,007 in Inner London, £17,953 for Outer London, £16,106 in the London fringe area), but as it is a salary it is taxed.

Teach First trainees receive a training salary on point 3 of the unqualified teachers' salary scale for the first year of their course, currently £18,629 (£22,522 in Inner London, £21,470 in Outer London and £19,620 in the London fringe area), and a newly qualified teacher's salary for the second year, currently £20,627 (£25,000 in Inner London, £24,000 in Outer London and £21,619 in the London fringe area).

Trying to decide which course

You need to take so many things into consideration when trying to make up your mind which kind of course best suits your needs. To help you to decide, you might like to consider the following points:

◆ Is money a problem? If so, you may just have to choose the course that makes it convenient for you to live at home (if you have not got a degree), or one of the employment-based courses (if you have).

◆ Your qualifications and experience may limit or increase your options.

◆ What do you most want from the higher education? Do you want to study your chosen subject(s) in depth or would you prefer to spend more time getting teaching experience and learning the technicalities of teaching? For the former you might choose a degree and then a year of PGCE or GTP, and a B.Ed. for the latter.

◆ How do you yourself learn best? Some students love the study aspect of the course and enjoy immersing themselves in books to extend their knowledge and understanding of the philosophical aspect of teaching, and so they might prefer the B.Ed. option. Others, who learn more quickly from practical experience, are more likely to prefer the degree and PGCE or GTP option.

◆ Do you thrive on pressure? The one-year postgraduate courses are probably the tougher option as you have to compress so much into under a year and learn quickly from your mistakes. If you prefer a less steep learning curve, the B.Ed. is probably the more comfortable because you have more time to redo things and to put into practice what you have been taught or else improve upon what you have done.

◆ If you follow the B.Ed. option, you will have a longer period to concentrate on teaching per se. The PGCE and GTTP options are really only ten months of training, after you exclude the summer holidays. They are very intensive, and some people believe that at the end you are possibly not as well prepared as the B.Ed. teachers, who have studied and trained for four years.

I believe that because a great deal of your performance is reliant on your personal qualities of patience, creativity, understanding of pupils' difficulties, organizational skills and ability to relate well to other people, the difference is not huge. By the time you have completed the induction year, it is probable that any difference in the effect of the two courses will have evened out.

If you want to teach in a secondary school, having a degree in your chosen subject is important as you will be concentrating solely on that subject or allied subjects for the rest of your teaching career. A large body of knowledge and understanding is essential for a teacher who may be expected to teach up to A level standard. Most B.Ed. teachers work in primary schools, and secondary teachers are more likely to have a degree and postgraduate training.

Also, the training salary for the PGCE is a tremendous bonus for those who want to start reducing their debts after graduation.

The graduate teacher programme
The graduate teacher programme differs from a PGCE in that it is school based. Graduates spend an academic year working mostly in school with some time in college. They have another placement of a few weeks in a different school so that they have a wider perspective on the range of schools in the UK.

This is an option often preferred by graduates who have done something else before deciding to join the teaching profession. It allows you a lot of opportunity to practise your teaching skills but far less time to study the theory and less opportunity to reflect on successful practice and discuss issues with lecturers and other students.

As with the PGCE, there is a steep learning curve as you have less than a year to learn everything that the B.Ed. student has to learn in four years, but it is reasonable to expect graduates to learn more quickly because they have already had the experience of completing a degree. On this course you can be thrown in at the deep end fairly quickly.

The right college or university
It is most important to choose the right college or university, particularly if you are starting a four-year course, because if you make

the wrong choice you are stuck with it. You need to be confident that you can feel happy in the atmosphere and that there are plenty of other activities for you to enjoy, because it is rare for teachers to succeed in changing their course from one college to another.

It is vital to attend an open day at each of the colleges or universities to which you apply and make sure you talk to students who attend the college, or have just left it, because they can give you a greater insight into what it is really like than you will obtain from a glossy brochure or any lecturer addressing the crowd of applicants.

Much of the advice that follows could apply to students contemplating any college or university course, not just teacher training. Draw up a list of the things that are important to you, taking into account each of the following.

The structure and content of the course itself

All teaching courses have to cover a core curriculum, which is English, maths and science, but some will be specializing in certain subjects.

Does it contain enough of the subjects that interest you? Remember that if you want to be a primary teacher, you will have to study a bit of every subject on the curriculum. A few hours spent studying the syllabus of each course is time well spent.

Support for the student

Most colleges and universities have student support services such as student counselling services, vocational guidance and a health centre. Teacher training courses can be very tough if you are assigned to a challenging school for teaching practice. Finding yourself working with children who are socially disadvantaged through poverty, homelessness or distress in the home can be a severe shock to the system for students who have had little contact with social problems in their lives.

Most colleges take seriously their responsibility of supporting students who are given difficult classes without guidance on how to deal with them, and should take steps to make sure the student is properly supported in the school. Don't be afraid to ask at your interview how often you will see your college supervisor while on teaching practice and how he or she would support you if you were having a hard time.

Prospects after qualifying

Don't forget there are college and university league tables publicizing what percentage of students get jobs after leaving. Since most colleges and universities advise students to look at school league tables before they apply for a job in a school, the same rule must apply to themselves. Obviously there is no point in spending a few years working hard unless there is a strong chance of your getting a teaching job at the end of it.

Prospects of getting a job vary from place to place and for different subjects. For example, science teachers are scarce in some parts of the country, such as London. Other areas have a need for more teachers in maths and ICT. In Northern Ireland there is a huge surplus of teachers and most have to take supply jobs for some time, until they can get a permanent post.

The location of the college or university

If you are already married or have children or both, your priority will be to study somewhere close to home. This could severely limit your choice. If you have more than one relevant institution within reasonable travelling distance, you may have to balance up your real choice against the time spent on travelling. Always work out how much time is needed to do the journey in the rush hour. You could try a dummy run each way. Remember, having two hours a day of unnecessary travelling will generate stress and lessen the quality of life for you and your family.

If you are young and single, it is often beneficial to leave home completely, money permitting. Coping on your own in a new place is a beneficial experience, and competent teachers are usually independent people who can stand securely on their own two feet. People grow up more quickly when they are not depending on their parents for daily moral and practical support.

The college environment

It is imperative that you like the feel of the college environment. Environment has a strong effect on behaviour and mood, and it would be disappointing to arrive and find your college in a dismal area with few amenities and poor public transport.

When you go for your interview, make sure a detailed trip of the whole environment is included. Don't forget to check the glossy pictures in the brochure against the reality of the campus. Remember that everywhere looks different on a wet day in winter from how it looks on the sunny day in the photograph.

The wider environment

Look at the town or city and what it has to offer by way of culture and leisure activities. Large cities are usually brimming with interesting places to go, but if you are considering studying in a small town or suburban area, it is important to check the local transport for the evenings and weekends.

Also, you need to check that it is a safe place in which to go out in the evenings. A small number of colleges are located in areas where it is foolish to go out at night on foot, even in a group. If you attend one of these, it is imperative to have a car or enough money to pay regular taxi or minicab fares. This is not an exaggeration. I know one young student who, with his friends, suffered a senseless beating from a gang of thugs who did not bother to steal their wallets or mobile phones.

Accommodation

It is important to get your accommodation fixed up well in advance of starting your course, preferably with the help of your university. I have known students to have a miserable first term, frantically looking for affordable accommodation that is not slummy, and within reasonable travelling distance of their college. Some universities and colleges have enough accommodation in halls of residence for all of their students for the duration of their course; others have enough for all their students for part of it. Try to find one that organizes accommodation for the first year at least, and enquire about how students find housing for the rest.

The advantages of living in college halls are that they are usually convenient to the college, geared up for the students' needs, and there are lots of students together so they make friends quickly. Many provide meals, which breaks you into your new life gently.

It is vitally important to ask to be shown around the college halls when you go for your interview because some are very old and dilapidated. I have known students to withdraw their application on seeing the college halls.

Extra-curricular facilities

Check the clubs and societies section of the brochure to ensure there are enough that interest you. Most colleges have a wide variety.

Also look closely at their facilities. An athletics club will never be first-rate unless it has a proper 400 metres stadium and field equipment, and a dramatic society is greatly enhanced by an attractive theatre with effective acoustics and up-to-date lighting and sound equipment.

Remember that your job opportunities are greatly enhanced if you can provide music, drama and sports activities.

Living expenses

Even if they take holiday jobs, most students have to take out a low-interest loan from the Student Loan Company to cover their living expenses. This does not have to be paid back until you start earning, and at least some of it may not have to be paid back at all if you are eligible for the Repayment of Teachers' Loans scheme.

The loan system has the disadvantage that students leave university with a mountain of debt around their neck, but nonetheless many students say it is better than having no university education at all.

A small number are fortunate enough to have parents who bankroll them for the duration of their course. If you are in this happy position, it is a smart move to take out a loan anyway and invest the money in a tax-free Individual Savings Account or Premium Bonds, keep the interest or winnings and pay the loan back at your leisure. This is perfectly legal, but, if you are following this advice, it is sensible not to mention it to students who are struggling with finances, because it is irritating for those who cannot do it.

In certain teaching jobs where there is a shortage, a fraction of the loan is wiped out each year that you teach in a maintained school and so you make an even greater gain.

Other students have parents who would like to help but are unable to do so. Sometimes they help by telling their sons or daughters to take out a loan and they will help them to pay it off when the time comes.

Useful contact information

◆ www.tta.gov.uk/fundingfortrainees
◆ DfES Student Support free information line: 0800 731 9133
◆ Teaching Information line: 0845 6000 991, or 0845 6000 992 for Welsh speakers. Fax: 0117 915 6578
◆ Your own local education authority (LEA). Ask for the department for student support for student teachers.

2 | Getting onto the course

Think ahead

If you are still at school

Start your planning early by remembering that many colleges will not consider you unless you have some experience of working with children or teenagers. Have you been a Sunday school teacher, Cub, Scout or Brownie leader or a youth worker in any local community centre? Did you have responsibility for running any school club or Combined Cadet activities? Have you been a captain of any sports club in school or out of it? These all show that you can take responsibility for organizing young people. Mentioning any of these on the form will enhance your chances of acceptance.

If you have done any of these things in school, it is worth writing them down and passing your list, as an aide-memoire, to the person who writes your reference. He or she unlikely to resent your doing so; in fact, the person will have so much to remember that he or she will probably be glad of your help.

If you already have a degree

If you already have a degree and are applying for a place on a postgraduate course, it is almost essential to have had some experience of working in a school. This means finding a friend who works in a school – it doesn't have to be a teacher – and contacting the headteacher and asking whether you can work in the school voluntarily for a week or two. It is easier if you have someone on the inside to introduce you because heads have got to be extremely careful about whom they allow into their school.

Alternatively, most universities have an afternoon each week with no lectures. Some undergraduates contact a local school and offer to spend that afternoon every week working there voluntarily. This is sensible, not just to impress the selection panel but to let you see that the classroom can look very different from the other side of the school desk. Many young people, particularly those who have attended well-equipped schools in affluent areas, are unaware of the challenges presented in schools with high turnovers of staff because of the pressures of coping with large classes or high percentages of children with special needs, very little spoken English, or the obstacles to learning imposed by poverty, disturbance and distress in the home.

By mentioning your awareness of the extra challenges that schools face, you are demonstrating your insight into the issues involved in being a successful teacher. That is bound to impress.

I know several graduates who before doing their one-year postgraduate study actually worked full time as unqualified teachers in private schools or international schools abroad. Obviously this was a safe passport onto the course.

Applying to the college or university

Don't limit yourself to one college or university; apply for several and wait for the conditional offers. You will probably have to apply through the Universities and Colleges Admissions Service (UCAS), but teachers in your school will be able to advise you. When offers arrive, it is tempting to put the lowest offer down as your first choice, but it is better to put the one you really prefer first, because once you have put a college or university as first, you are expected to stick to that choice even if you have good enough grades for your second choice.

Graduates applying for the PGCE course apply through the Graduate Teacher Training Registry.

Filling in the form

Often students are so keen to set the wheels in motion that they fill in the form and send it off without taking time to consider all the fine tuning.

Try to keep at the front of your mind that most universities are not scratching around looking for students to fill their places; they have far more applicants than they could possibly accommodate, so you need to make your application as near to perfect as you possibly can, to maximize your chances. Here are a few hints:

♦   Always photocopy the form before you start and write a couple of practice copies before you write the one you intend to send off.

◆ This is the first impression they have of you, so the form must be neat and word perfect. Typing, where possible, is best, unless the form says that it has to be in your own handwriting.

◆ Bear in mind that although supply and demand for college places is also a factor, no college will accept anyone they consider unsuitable just to fill up their places.

◆ If you are still at school, your careers teacher should be willing to look over a draft of your application form before you write the final copy and send it off. He or she can often suggest small improvements.

◆ Keep a copy of the form to use in preparation for your interview and to have as a basis for filling in the next one.

The student's statement is the most important part. The selection panel are looking for students who are absolutely certain they want to be teachers. Say why you want to be a teacher – why you have enjoyed working with children or teenagers; who or what inspired you. You got satisfaction out of helping them to learn/progress/develop skills. Mention that it has widened your horizon, making you more aware of the difficulties they face, and has given you the urge to make a difference.

The interview

It is vital for the universities' and colleges' admissions panels to be certain that the students they accept are absolutely sure that they want to teach because they do not want their course statistics to be spoiled by a high drop-out rate. They look for evidence of commitment to the profession, and lip-service is not enough. Some lecturers say that they are looking for students who have demonstrated commitment to children as well as their subject and are more likely to accept students who have experience of working with children or teenagers.

This is your chance to enlarge on all your experience of working with young people. They will like it if you speak enthusiastically, making it clear that you have benefited from the experience. Tell them what skills you have developed: organizing trips, coping with critical parents, teaching children to sort out conflicts, managing behaviour of children with problems, supporting them through anxiety about exams, adolescence, parents separating. You can't work with children for long without learning something from them, and you should demonstrate this.

Similarly, if you are a graduate hoping to do a PGCE or GTP next, the admissions panel will be impressed if you describe work that you have done successfully while working voluntarily in a school.

The interview panel is looking for potential teachers who also possess the following qualities, not necessarily in this order:

◆ good health
◆ an even keener interest in children and teenagers than in their subject
◆ the ability to sustain long hours of pressure
◆ inventiveness of mind
◆ self-confidence
◆ the ability to stand up for themselves strongly but without aggression
◆ intelligence
◆ patience
◆ tolerance
◆ sensitivity
◆ the ability to work cooperatively with adults and children of all classes, creeds, colours and levels of ability.

They have half an hour to find out how many of these qualities you possess, and you have half an hour to persuade them you have all or most of them.

A few guidelines

Interviews differ from college to college. In some they are very formal and you are quizzed by a small panel of lecturers. Others are quite informal and relaxed. Some students have told me that the interviewer appeared to be just trying to get to know them.

The following points may be helpful:

◆ Look smart. Even in these liberal times, many lecturers still think it is important. You can of course revert to a casual appearance for the rest of your college career, except teaching practice.
◆ Hold your head up and your shoulders back and look them confidently in the eye.
◆ If you are nervous, try to hide it. They are looking for self-assured people.
◆ Don't mumble. A clear voice that is pleasant to the ear is an important attribute for a teacher.

◆ Never fabricate or exaggerate your experience. If you are caught out, you will definitely be turned down.

Preparation

You should always prepare for an interview because there is nothing more disheartening than coming out of one and thinking of answers you could have given. Before you go, you should ask yourself what questions you would ask if you were the interviewer. Forewarned is forearmed. If you know people who have recently had similar interviews, ask them what questions they were asked and prepare by writing down the questions and adding model answers.

Ask a friend to take your notes and give you a practice interview the night before. I always find this preparation enhances my performance for any sort of interview. Read your notes an hour or less before you go in. Here are a few questions to practise. You can choose the answer you think best or prepare your own.

Q   'Why do you want to be a teacher?'
A   'I have a keen interest in children/the promotion of skills and knowledge.'
A   'I want a rewarding job.'
A   'I once had a superb teacher who was so enthusiastic and was clearly thriving on her success, and s/he inspired me to enter the profession.'
A   'Teaching is in my family, so I do know all the drawbacks as well as the good points.'

Q   'What is your experience of children?'
A   'I have worked with youth groups, Sunday school, holiday play schemes, sports clubs, Combined Cadets.' [They may pick something interesting out of your application form. This is your chance to elaborate on everything you have done.]
A   'I have children of my own, babysat for others, got loads of younger brothers/sisters/cousins.'

Q   'How has this influenced your decision to be a teacher?'
A   'I enjoy working with them.'
A   'I take pleasure in watching them learn, develop, mature, acquire new skills.'
A   'Although my parents, who are teachers, complain about the stresses and strains of the job, I notice that they also get a lot of pleasure out of it and don't seem to want to give it up.'

Q 'What skills and qualities does a teacher need?'

A 'An inventive mind, the ability to cope with people of all sorts, organizational skills, a wide body of knowledge [primary], a deep knowledge and understanding of their subject [secondary], patience [all age groups], enthusiasm, endurance, thick skin, ability to think ahead, think of several things at once, think on one's feet, flexibility.'

Q 'Which is the more important, organizational skills or patience with pupils?'

A 'Organizational skills. If you are not well organized, it is easier for pupils to become disorganized/uninterested and then you will need even more patience to regain their attention.'

Or

A 'Patience. A good relationship with pupils is the bedrock of successful teaching. Pupils need above all to know that their teachers care about them, have the time and patience to listen to them.'

A 'Both are extremely important. It would be hard to pick between them.' (Then mention the reasons for both. A lecturer will not mind your having a different opinion from his or her own as long as you can back it up with logical reasoning.)

Q 'What are your leisure-time activities?' [They should be on the form.]

A Have a long list ready. They are looking for all-round people. Expand on your answer by telling them why it is such a valuable skill. For example, if you have a talent for music, point out how it makes you use both halves of the brain. If you are keen on sports, elaborate on the health aspect. Explain how you could use your knowledge and skills in school, for example for extra-curricular activities.

Q 'How do you think you will cope with being alone with children for most of a working day?'

A 'I shall enjoy the challenge.' [Although it is fashionable, I hate that word 'challenge'. It's the current buzzword used in such a way to suggest that it is a panacea.]

A 'I find it fascinating to watch them interacting and developing.'

Q 'How would you inspire a love of your subject in your pupils?' [Secondary]

A   'Build up a positive relationship with them and make sure I deliver lessons that are interesting and involve them in active learning.'

A   'Try to make the subject relevant to them and to what interests them.' For example, maths teachers can make up problems about calculating angles on a football pitch, English teachers make sure they make available plenty of books that appeal to the pupils' age group. History comes alive when children visit historical sites and take part in historical activities. Introduce drama into lessons; children love to perform and have everyone's attention.

Q   'When did you last read/how well informed are you about the National Curriculum document for your subject?' [Secondary. If you are still at school, you could ask one of your teachers to lend you a copy of the document to read before your interview. If you have left school, you can acquire one from the Department for Children, Schools and Families orderline, Sanctuary Buildings, Great Smith Street, London SW1P 3BT. Telephone: 0845 602 2260. www.dcsf.gov.uk.]

Q   'Why is the National Curriculum important?'

A   'It provides some uniformity within the system, so that pupils going off to secondary school have had a similar foundation for their secondary teachers to build upon. It also ensures that schools do not leave blank spots in their pupils' knowledge, even though some schools may be able to achieve a higher standard or cover more ground than others.'

Q   'What aspects of the National Curriculum do you find stimulating/ unstimulating?' [Whatever your main subject, you could adapt a few of these or think up your own.]

A   'I like parts that involve the pupil finding out things for themselves, such as planning and carrying out science experiments, reading historical documents, maths investigations.'

A   'I like National Curriculum topics that are relevant to normal everyday life, like studying the effects humans have on the environment and the need to conserve the Earth's resources.'

A   'Learning languages is so satisfying because it enables you to get more out of your holidays abroad by being able to communicate with the people.'

A   'I like topics that involve hands-on activities like recycling paper in the classroom. Visiting museums or villages (like Blist's Hill

Victorian village) where pupils have the opportunity to experience a past way of life is tremendously stimulating.'

A   'I am not so keen on topics that are purely theoretical and don't seem relevant to me and my everyday life. For example, I have learned lots of topics in maths that I cannot use.' [You can add a philosophical comment about the difficulty of producing a National Curriculum that would interest all pupils in all topics, and realizing that it is a teacher's job to make the curriculum interesting and relevant to pupils.]

Sometimes the panel give a group of applicants a piece to read and then initiate a group discussion about the article with a lecturer there to supervise. This can be difficult as some people will try to get themselves noticed by dominating the discussion, excluding others. Fortunately, lecturers are aware of this and are able to give all the students the chance to express their opinions. If you find yourself taking part in this sort of activity, don't be afraid to speak up. It doesn't matter whether the lecturer agrees with you or not. Lecturers want to know whether you have got ideas and confidence, and can show that you are a thinking person.

When the A level results come out

As with any university application it is vital to be at home, or at least within immediate computer access, when the results come out. Remember, you may need to go to an interview at short notice, so if you really cannot be at home, you should not be far away, or at the very least within easyJet or Ryanair (or other budget airline) travelling distance.

Don't despair if you do not have the grades for your preferred college. You must log onto the website immediately to find out whether you have been accepted anyway, because often, if they have enough places, they will take students with a lesser grade, especially if those students have had a successful interview. If not, you can telephone them quickly and tell them you are still interested. They will tell you whether there is any chance, and you will have to either wait in hope for a day or two or contact Clearing. If you have reasonably good results and are willing to be flexible about where you go, you may very well still get a place if you follow Clearing's procedure. For details, go to www.ucas.com/clearing.

If you have got the right grades, you must contact the college or university at once to accept the place.

The pre-course placement

If you are a graduate and you have been accepted for the GTP or PGCE course, your college will most probably ask you to spend a week in a school before you start your teacher training. This is to give you the chance to make absolutely certain you like it, to get the feel of the job and, hopefully, pick up a few tips.

The pre-course placement is time well spent because some people decide after a week of grief that it is not for them, and so save themselves a lot of trouble. I know one graduate who withdrew her application from the course because she was deterred by the staffroom politics alone. Unfortunately, some do not discover that teaching is not their cup of tea until they have gone a term or two into the course, causing wasted time and effort all round.

You will have to organize this pre-course placement for yourself. The best way is through a teacher whom you know, but if you do not know any whom you feel you can approach, just try a few schools in your area and ask. It is sensible to call in at the school and ask in person whether you can spend a week there, because heads understandably can be wary of allowing strangers in. It is a good idea to bring your college's letter with you, partly so that the head knows what they want you to do and partly for identification. If the head has any doubts, he or she can telephone the college.

Most schools are amenable to allowing a potential teacher to spend a week with them, and some are only too happy to welcome an extra pair of hands. Of course, you must always dress smartly before you go, as first impressions are important.

On the placement week, some start to have doubts and are uncertain whether they should continue. If you find yourself in this position, don't make a rash decision that you might later regret. Remember that there is a wide variety of primary and secondary schools and you might just have been unlucky. You could contact another school and ask to pass a week there.

Try to keep it at the front of your mind that there is no such thing as a typical school. There are private schools with small classes, the best equipment and supportive parents; and rough schools with a large number of challenges posed by poverty, low staffing levels and poor management. There is also every combination in between. A change of school might completely transform your view.

If you can, it is worth trying to spend longer than a week in a school and/or do some other type of work with children in a holiday play scheme or youth group. To do this you could ring up your LEA and ask whether they run holiday play schemes or can tell you of any. You could also visit your local library to see what is available locally. Sometimes churches organize activities for children, but these are voluntary and you might need something that pays.

Tips on coping with your placement

Keeping your path smooth
◆ As soon as you arrive, go straight to the head to introduce yourself if you have not already met him or her and thank the head for allowing you to come.
◆ On the first day, wear something neutral in the clothes department and then adapt according to the school's dress code, because it is irritating for teachers if they find that visitors can get away with something they can't.
◆ Fairly soon, ask whom to pay for tea and coffee and pay up-front.
◆ Try to get on with everyone and avoid staffroom politics.
◆ Volunteering to do playground duty will improve your welcome.
◆ If they have any fund-raising or evening events that week, offer to turn up and help.
◆ Keep your negative comments to yourself. Teachers tend to withdraw their help quite quickly when you rub them up the wrong way.

Behaving like a professional
◆ You might hear staff talking about pupils. It is important to respect the confidentiality of all such information.
◆ Don't be afraid to ask about anything you don't understand; no one blames you for wanting to learn. On the other hand, don't bombard teachers with questions.
◆ If a pupil makes a negative comment about a member of staff, you can sidestep by changing the subject. It is unwise to allow yourself to be drawn into an argument.
◆ Stay well out of any heated staffroom discussions.
◆ After you leave, write a letter of thanks to the head and any teacher who has been particularly helpful.

Being sensitive to the teachers

At certain times, teachers are under more pressure than others. If there is an Ofsted inspection taking place, be aware that they do not have so much time to devote to helping you. Also, in periods of marking exam papers and writing reports, teachers are often tired and stressed.

Understanding the background

If you plan to do the PGCE for teaching in a secondary school, you might be asked to do your placement in a primary school. This is really a good idea, because it gives you the chance to:

◆ get a feel for a primary-school atmosphere so you know the children's previous experience
◆ see the level of work that pupils can achieve at the top end of the primary school, to give you a better idea of what you can expect from them in their first year in secondary, remembering that this will vary from school to school
◆ note the level of maturity of pupils at the top end of the primary school

Remember that to teach in a secondary school, you need a wide range of personal skills because you have to teach children, hormonal adolescents and young adults.

How to get the most out of the placement

It is now recognized that even experienced teachers learn a lot by observing the efficient practice of others. In fact, in some schools teachers are encouraged to spend some time in other classes observing their colleagues. You will probably enjoy sitting in classrooms observing how teachers work, picking up ideas and, if it is some time since you were at school yourself, musing about how much things have changed.

Before you go into a classroom, remember that some teachers, even competent, experienced ones, can be self-conscious and might not actually want you there. Try to be sensitive. If they seem less than pleased about your presence, it is worth making an admiring remark about the displays on the wall and asking whether there is anything you can do to help or where it is most convenient for you to sit.

A positive, supportive attitude and willingness to work and learn go a long way with most teachers. And, of course, always thank them before you move on to the next class.

What to look for while observing a lesson

The staff–pupil relationship plays a large part in the quality of work for both the pupils and the teacher. Relationships often reflect the personality of the head. Those heads who are efficient and treat the staff even-handedly and with appreciation tend to have a staffroom full of people who extend the same goodwill to their colleagues and pupils. The set of rules by which the staff treat each other and the pupils is sometimes called the hidden curriculum. You might want to look at it, as well as the teacher's behaviour management techniques and methods of organizing the class to learn. Try observing these points.

Managing the pupils
◆ Is the atmosphere calm, strained, pressurized, happy, hostile?
◆ Behaviour management skills – how does the teacher control the pupils?
◆ Are the pupils switched on or off, on task, involved in the learning activities?
◆ If you look at a lesson where the pupils are not switched on and one where they are, ask yourself what causes the difference. Is it the lesson content, the way it is presented, the activities that the pupils do, the teacher's relationship with the pupils or a mixture of two or more of these?
◆ How does the teacher coax the less interested pupils to take part?

Delivering the lessons
◆ Look at the overall structure of lessons. Watch how the warm-up, main part of the lesson and plenary all fit together and flow into each other.
◆ How is the lesson organized? Is the teacher doing all the work and the pupils sitting passively? Are they working independently, or in groups cooperatively? Or is there a mixture of these?
◆ Are the pupils aware of the objective of the lesson and has the teacher achieved it? That is, have the pupils grasped the concept, or developed the skill? Do they understand the information that was the point of the lesson?

If you are concentrating on a lot of the details above, it becomes hard to keep it all in your head, particularly if you are changing classes, so it is worth keeping a notepad handy to make notes of things that look helpful for the future, such as points concerning behaviour management techniques or methods of teaching. You can't have too many of either.

Most teachers are happy about this, but if the teacher looks dismayed about your taking notes in his or her lesson, smile and say something like, 'Thank you for that. I've picked up a few tips and jotted them down.' Try to look eager and non-judgemental. Don't look like an inspector.

Other things to do
Most of these can apply to either primary or secondary school.

◆ Sit in on lessons for as many different age groups as you can, to get a wide picture.

◆ If you are in the school on the first day of term in September, try to find an experienced teacher who will allow you to sit in on his or her first lesson with a new class. The first contact lesson is the most important lesson of the week because the teacher establishes the foundation of his or her relationship with the new class. Some teachers like this time alone with a new class, but if you can sit in on one, you might learn something about establishing a positive relationship.

◆ Try to spend some time in the youngest and oldest classes, to give you an idea of the range of the school.

◆ Go to assembly every day because assemblies vary enormously even within one school. Attending assemblies lets you see what appeals to children and it might give you some ideas.

◆ Offer to help with marking of the class lesson you have just observed, because it gives you a better view of the range of children's ability. If the teacher doesn't want an unqualified person marking the books, ask whether you can just look at them to get an idea of what the pupils can do.

◆ If you are in the same class for a few sessions and are feeling confident, you may ask the teacher whether you could take part or all of a lesson, or help a group of less able pupils.

◆ Ask whether you can sit in on the planning meeting.

◆ Offer to hear the children read, or read a story to the class (primary). You can learn a lot by observing, but there is nothing like practical experience to help you learn to do the job properly.

◆ Have a look at the National Curriculum documents for your subject (secondary) or age range (primary). It's never too soon to start accumulating information.

This should be a stimulating week for you. Hopefully, it will give you ideas for the age range you want to teach and the type of teacher you want to be.

When you start college or university

When you start your course you will probably be given an opportunity to discuss the placement with lecturers and other students and be given some follow-up focused tasks to get you to think about what you learned during the placement. For example, one task might be directed at ensuring that you are familiar with the transition period before pupils come to secondary school. It will be easier to relate to them if you know where they are coming from.

You may be asked what you have learned from your visit and what benefit it had for you. You will be asked to describe how things were done in the class (or classes) and analyse how effective those things were. How you describe and comment on the effectiveness of the teachers you observed and how efficiently the school provided for the pupils' needs will give your lecturers a fair idea of how well you are engaging in finding out about the complexities of the job. Try to keep at the front of your mind that during this discussion the lecturer is trying to find out about you, not the school.

Early on in the course you may have an assignment about pre-course placement as part of your professional studies course. For example, you might be asked to explain the system set up for dealing with children with special needs, and discuss its effectiveness.

Hopefully, you will enjoy the placement, and find it an interesting and stimulating start to the course.

3 | Getting through the course

Freshers' week

Freshers' week is the first week at any college or university, whether it is for teacher training or for some other degree. If you have left school within the previous year, Freshers' week can be a stimulating experience. You can finally throw off the 'school kid' image and step into the adult world.

For 18-year-old students who have left home for the first time, there might be a mixture of enthusiasm and nervous anticipation. Some may be trying to hide their homesickness. Those who arrive at a college from overseas and do not know anyone can find it nerve-racking to find themselves suddenly alone and away from home.

For the younger students, the first priority is to get to know the other students to make friends. Friends are the people who will support and encourage you through the pressure of exams, writing essays and dissertations, and teaching practice. Do not underestimate their importance. Young people feeling unsure of themselves are sometimes tempted to try to impress their peers. This often antagonizes others who are not feeling confident, and the façade falls apart quickly. You will make friends more quickly and keep them if you avoid putting on an act.

What goes on?

There will be a week of activities to help you familiarize yourself with the university and its routines, and find out who everyone is. It is a quick way to widen your circle of acquaintances and make friends.

Most students and lecturers to whom I spoke gave the following advice:

◆ It is best to attend every event, whether it is compulsory or not.
◆ Disregard any predetermined ideas given to you by others and go with an open mind.
◆ Students' clubs and societies vary from the highly intellectual to the trivial; from the debating and politics societies with their prestigious speakers to the Winnie-the-Pooh society. There will also be lots of different sports clubs, musical and dramatic societies, religious and cultural organizations. There is bound to be something that interests you.
◆ Make sure you join a few clubs to help you get into the swing of things, meet people and make friends. If you are shy of going alone at first, persuade someone to go with you. Other students may be only too glad of your company.
◆ This is also a time to learn about yourself. You may find all sorts of new things that interest you, and find that you have talents of which you were unaware.

The following advice is from students who have completed the PGCE or GTP courses:

◆ Be willing to immerse yourself in the course for the duration. If you are married, make sure your partner knows that you will not always be available to support him or her for the time of the course.
◆ Have an escape activity if you can – preferably something that is completely unrelated to the course.
◆ Some students on one-year courses told me the trainees had widely varying attitudes. There may be some who are not taking it seriously and who will deliberately or inadvertently bring others down with them by depressing them with negative attitudes or trying to distract them from their work by suggesting something more interesting to do than go to lectures. Don't let them wreck your chances. Give them a wide berth.

Lectures

Lectures take different forms. Sometimes there are a hundred or more students in a lecture theatre and you are not allowed to ask questions unless invited. So instead make a practice of taking notes and jotting down questions to ask in your seminar group or tutorial group.

In others there is more interaction between the lecturer and students. Although it is tempting to sit in lectures just soaking up all the information and taking notes, it is also wise to ask questions when you can, to get the best out of them. It is exactly the same as the school classroom situation.

Most students told me that the best lectures are the ones that are geared up to what you are about to do, such as lectures on teaching practice just before you do it, to give you ideas, or lectures on subjects that you have chosen for an essay or assignment. Others said they gained a lot from the lectures that came after the placement because the theory had turned to practice and now made sense to them.

Lectures where there is interaction between the lecturer and students or students and other students and active participation by students are most productive.

Some students find the lectures interesting and helpful. Some find a high correlation between the theory and the practice while others complain that they are a waste of time because they only want to get out into the schools and start teaching.

The content of the lecture may seem too far removed from your immediate needs but remember it is a long time before you will retire, and information and ideas flowing today may well come in useful one day.

You must always remember there are many ways to do everything, and lecturers are giving you suggestions that will work with all classes some of the time and some classes all of the time. But don't fall into the trap of thinking that anything works with all classes all of the time. You will eventually need to experiment and find out which methods you find easiest to use, and develop the skill of finding new methods for yourself.

Everyone accepts that the experience in the school far outweighs the value of the theory, but don't underestimate the theory. Knowledge is power, and you can't have too much of it.

Being organized

Remember that your information is useful only when it is readily accessible. Keep your notes carefully because the subject of a lecture may come up in the classroom several months later when you thought you had forgotten it. It is time-economic to invest in sets of file dividers for your ring binders and arch-lever folders, with the contents of each section clearly marked and your pages numbered. The small amount of time spent on setting up the system at the beginning can save you a lot of time later on when you need information quickly. Lecturers say that students waste a lot of time through being disorganized. Remember, lost time means added stress.

Getting the most value out of lectures

It is surprising how much agreement there was between lecturers and students to whom I spoke about this. Here is a précis of what they said:

◆ Always approach lectures with an open mind. Don't allow yourself to be thrown by new ideas. Be willing to try out new things in the classroom.

◆ Lecturers with long years of experience have ideas and beliefs of their own. You can accept their ideals or reject them as you wish, but only after you have thought about them, not before.

◆ Try not to switch off, even if you do not agree, or feel bored or tired. Engage with lecturers, for if you don't, you will probably grow into the type of teacher who cannot engage with the pupils.

◆ Few lecturers, if any, profess to know it all. Most accept that there are many ways to teach and learn. They are unlikely to object to your questioning their ideas and suggestions, and frequently welcome students with an enquiring mind. So don't be afraid to speak up and debate with them.

◆ In lectures, avoid sitting near those who are not interested and want to have their own little chat to pass the time. That means sitting near the front, for they will be at the back.

◆ If you can't avoid them, feel free to ask them to save their chat for later as they are spoiling the lecture for those of you who are interested and do want to learn. Students are often wary of speaking out, afraid that they will be accused of being 'swots', but other students who are also irritated by them will thank you for it and probably admire you for shutting them up.

◆ Asking questions during lectures when it is allowed helps you to get the most out of them. It is similar to the situation for the pupils in a classroom: they learn more when they are actively involved.

◆ If you do not feel confident enough to speak up in a lecture, you might instead discuss the subject with other students to see whether they agree with you. Don't worry if you cannot quickly draw conclusions about what works best. It takes discussion and experience to decide what methods work best for you.

Essays

Many students dislike writing essays because they find it tedious and too far removed from the practice of the classroom. Eager for hands-on experience, they complain that writing essays is a waste of time. Don't get caught out by having that attitude. To the experienced teacher or lecturer it sounds arrogant.

The old maxim – what you put in is what you get out of it – applies here. There are usually lots of essays to write covering a range of topics, about which you might in some cases have a choice. Some are subject based and some are related to issues that arise in school, such as bullying. Other popular topics are inclusion in education, differentiation, behaviour management and assessment policies. Essays on any of these topics can be specific to individual academic subjects.

This is an opportunity for you to do your own research in the library and read various papers on the topic to draw conclusions and form opinions of your own. Although it may seem like pure theory when you are writing the essay, your research gives you a chance to find out about best practice and refine your ideas.

Some students complain that writing essays is a waste of time, but it is important to think long-term. The information may not be useful immediately, but during the years that follow, you will find that the job is so long, wide and varied that you cannot have too much information. In fact, I have known advisory teachers to say that when you think you know it all, it is time to give up because you are clearly past it.

Tips on essay writing

- Always choose a topic that interests you.
- Look closely at the list of Professional Standards for Qualified Teacher Status (QTS). Is there a topic that you could study to show that you are aware of it and understand all its implications? Try examining all of the standards of Q10 to Q21 in the section on Knowledge and Understanding. There are lots of possibilities there to demonstrate your awareness of educational issues and, hopefully, fulfil the criteria of the standards as well.
- Avoid 'essay crisis' at all costs. Start reading as soon as you can after receiving the question. A last-minute job is never your best.
- Read a lot of literature before you begin writing, because different books, Department for Children, Schools and Families (DCSF) documents and educational newspapers and magazines will give you different angles from which to look at issues, including ones that you had not thought of. Make a lot of notes.

◆ Talk informally to other people about the essay topic – your peers, your lecturers, teachers whom you know, even your children if they are at school and it is a relevant topic. Everyone has a viewpoint, and discussing issues sparks off ideas that you would otherwise have missed.

◆ Remember that before professional writers start writing, they spend a lot of time thinking about what they are going to write. After they have written it, they will probably leave it for a few days and then go back to it to improve it. The same rules should apply to you when writing your essay.

◆ The internet is useful, but never adequate on its own.

◆ It is tempting to cut and paste chunks from the internet and use them word for word, but foolish, because lecturers are bound to realize what you have done.

◆ Rather than piling up a mountain of notes, try using a dictating machine and just speak into it. It is much faster than writing or typing unless you are a competent typist. One student told me how she recorded some lectures on a mini tape recorder – a useful extra if your budget can stretch to it.

◆ Go through your written notes with a highlighter and mark what is relevant to your essay topic. This should cut down your notes quite drastically.

◆ Similarly, listen to your tape and make notes of the points that are relevant.

◆ Study the brief or question closely to make sure you have answered the question.

◆ Being concise is better than using a lot of extra words.

◆ Take essay deadlines seriously and deliver your essays on time to avoid that feeling of irritation when an essay is returned to you with the word 'LATE' in red letters on the front even though you have missed the deadline by minutes.

Assignments and projects

Assignments and projects are specific tasks to make practical investigations in order to find information. They are different from essays (and, I always found, more interesting) because as well as doing the background reading and making notes, you also have to carry out a test or experiment, make observations and/or record results, analyse the results and draw conclusions, which have to be presented with careful and reasoned argument or explanation.

How are assignments and projects helpful to the student?

Carrying out assignments involves more active learning than writing essays and so many students find it more beneficial. Having to draw your own conclusions based on information that you have found out for yourself helps you to formulate your own ideas with confidence, rather than merely accepting what you have read in a book.

Some assignments are time-consuming and so are not practical to carry out when you have a full-time teaching job. This is an opportunity to find out things that you will not have time to investigate in the future.

Most assignments are school based and concerned with looking at practice in the context of an authentic classroom. Students have the opportunity to find information about issues such as assessment, behaviour management, how pupils learn and how teachers can engage their interest.

As with the essays, you can kill two birds with one stone by looking at your list of Professional Standards for QTS and finding topics that will fulfil the criteria for some of them. Before choosing a subject, always check the document to see whether you can find an interesting subject that will fulfil one of the criteria from the list.

Lecturers tell me they make the activity useful to students by giving lots of constructive feedback. Where students make large errors of judgement, it is important to help them onto the right lines as early as possible. Try to see assignments as a long-term benefit. As with everything else you do at college, each item is likely to be of benefit some day.

Examples of assignments and projects

Assignments and projects vary in both subject and method. The following are examples given to me by recent students.

Observational assignments

One student told me of an assignment 'to examine teachers' interactions with pupils to find if there is a gender bias'. Some students observed teachers working and made tally charts of the interaction between female pupils and teachers, and male pupils and teachers, whether that interaction was initiated by the teacher or the pupil and whether it was negative or positive.

At the end of five or six lessons, some found that a startling 80 per cent or so of the interactions of both male and female teachers were with boys. It is important to learn from findings such as this that some members of the class take up a disproportionate amount of a teacher's time, so that you can guard against falling into a trap such as neglecting the girls. Some students' findings and conclusions could of course be different from those of other students. When you are carrying out this type of assignment, it is important when stating your conclusions to add a sentence or two acknowledging that your experiment or investigation was on a very small scale and so cannot be taken as necessarily representing the school population as a whole.

Examining the range of ability within one age group

Another type of assignment is when students are asked to carry out the same set of activities with a bright pupil, a moderately able one and one of lower ability of the same age group. At the end, you might see a staggeringly wide gulf between the lower end and the top end of the ability range in the class. From this you will learn the value of providing different levels of work for the different ability groups within the class.

It might make you aware that putting pupils into streamed classes for some subjects makes it easier to give pupils more attention because the teacher is not being stretched in all directions at once. You might also become aware of the value of providing a support teacher for less able pupils to work in a small group to help them to keep up with the class.

Finding ways of developing good practice

Another example might be to write a set of lesson plans for your main subject, make resources, deliver the lessons and evaluate them. When teaching a topic, say electricity, find out what difficulties the pupils have and how you could help to resolve those difficulties. What everyday activities can you devise to make the lesson more interesting for them and how would you improve it in the future? How can you make the topic relevant to their everyday life?

From this you learn that even the best-prepared lessons can go wrong and even the lessons that go well can be improved. The important part will be finding ways of preventing difficulties that you had not previously anticipated and thinking up interesting activities to make the lessons exciting.

This is an invaluable activity because it is what you will need to do when you are qualified, and your colleagues and pupils will appreciate your being able to do it well.

Focusing on developing skills across the curriculum

Some assignments are longer and students are given a topic to research over several weeks to find information and use it to produce a body of information and ideas. Examples might include finding ways in which pupils' learning can be improved by using ICT, or looking at ways in which lessons can be made accessible to children who are in the early stages of learning English, or have special needs.

This of course requires observation of teachers demonstrating good practice, and discussion with specialist teachers. Don't be afraid to pick their brains. You will also need to find opportunities to try out methods and see what works best for you.

Most students I spoke to found these 'hands-on' parts of the course interesting and helpful. Most emphasized the importance of choosing topics that were of particular interest to themselves.

Mock-up lessons in college

A mock-up lesson is one where students take turns in preparing a lesson to deliver to other students who role-play as pupils. Some students find this a nightmare at first. The confident and the extroverted find it enjoyable. Once you get used to it, you will probably find it helpful.

The advantages of mock-up lessons include the following:

◆ If you are feeling nervous about taking your first lessons, they are an opportunity to have some practice before being faced with the 'real thing'.

◆ You are forced to focus your mind on how to explain things clearly and lucidly so that pupils can understand.

◆ You get instant feedback from the lecturer and other students.

◆ In some colleges the lesson is videoed and played back, giving students the opportunity to view their own performance, make a self-assessment and listen to constructive suggestions for improvement.

There are disadvantages too:

◆ Some students find them daunting, even terrifying.

◆ They are not authentic; you do not actually have to take responsibility for the management of equipment and the pupils' safety and behaviour.

◆ They force students to focus on themselves as performers instead of the pupils as learners, but class teaching is also about the management of groups of learners; matching work to pupils' abilities, and managing resources and groups who can work in harmony. Even if you shine in the mock-up lesson, it is still possible that you will find the real thing difficult.

◆ Sometimes students do not take mock-up lessons seriously and, when role-playing as a pupil, they try to wind up the student delivering the lesson.

Exams

Exams are most important for the B.Ed. student because the results decide what class of degree you get, whereas your teaching practice will only be classified as a pass or fail. Some students complain that this system is heavily biased towards the academic, since students' ability to write essays does not always reflect their ability to relate well to pupils, manage their behaviour and facilitate their learning.

This system could make it tempting to do only the bare minimum necessary to pass your teaching practice, but it is better to think long-term because the more effort you put into your teaching practice, the easier it will be to cope with your induction year.

PART 2: TEACHING PRACTICE

The preparation

Teaching practice (TP) is the most stimulating and productive part of teacher training. In some colleges, students, quite profitably, spend much more time in school than in college. TP is also the part that gives you the clearest idea of how much you like the job and how well you can cope with it.

Although the class of your degree may be decided by your academic performance, making a success of teaching practices is also vital to passing the course. I have been told by lecturers that if they are uncertain whether to pass a student, they use the yardstick of whether they would want the student teaching their own son or daughter. A valid way to decide!

I have known many student teachers who have entered schools nervously for their first teaching practice and emerged at the end of it with renewed confidence. It is also the part of the course that causes a lot of students to have second thoughts. Many who drop out of the course do so after a bad experience of teaching practice.

One problem is that students come across irritations and difficulties that they had not anticipated. Sometimes this means having to do extra TP during the college holidays because they did not perform well enough or had time off when they found it stressful.

Some found nits in their hair, or had a miserable time after inadvertently offending the head or a class teacher. Some students find it more difficult than being a class teacher because working within someone else's framework can be so much more restrictive than creating your own.

Although many teachers are helpful and supportive towards students, a small number are unsympathetic and find them a nuisance because they create extra work and may accept a lower standard of work and behaviour than the class teacher, who then has the task of pulling the standard back up when the student leaves. Others take advantage of students and leave them to cope alone while they take unscheduled non-contact time.

I have known students to give up after working with unhelpful class teachers or heads of department on teaching practice while others, determined to cope, rose above the difficulties and emerged stronger. Many of the pitfalls could have been avoided with a little prior thought.

Protect yourself as well as the pupils

1. *Know the basic rules.* In almost every school there is a rule banning everyone from leaving children unsupervised by an adult. This is because they are not insured if they have an accident, and parents can sue for compensation. It is never worth taking the risk of leaving pupils alone, especially as it is more difficult for unions to defend you if you have broken the rules.

2. *Join a union or association.* It is wise to join the students' section of a teachers' union or professional association. If you are left in charge of pupils and one has an accident or, worse, makes an accusation against you, it is reassuring to know that legal advice is at the end of a telephone. Also, if the worst happens and a parent tries to prosecute you, there will be legal backing to prepare your case and defend you in court. Be sure to check before you join that this service is included.

Some colleges actually call in union representatives to advise students before they go to schools. Usually membership is free to students, and some teachers' unions and associations even give a reduced-fee membership when you start your induction year. Often students join two or three different organizations. In case your college does not provide you with the information, a list of unions and professional associations is given in Appendix 2 at the back of this book. This is a good time to look at what unions offer. Some have regular magazines and lively websites packed with advice for the student and newly qualified teacher. It is a good idea to look at them all before making a decision.

3. *Accusations and allegations.* Today we are living in a climate where we are more acutely aware of child abuse. If a child makes an accusation against a teacher, the teacher is often suspended until an investigation by the police has taken place. The same can apply to students on teaching practice.

Although it is rare for teachers to be charged, any teacher who has been wrongly accused has found the weeks of waiting an unbearable strain, and some have given up teaching because of it. Because it is so easy for children to make accusations, many heads and teachers advocate that you never allow yourself to be alone with a child. Accusations against teachers and students are hardly likely to succeed where there are witnesses to refute them.

In the past, an adult's word was always considered more reliable than a child's. Now the balance has shifted, so it is sensible never to allow yourself to be in such a vulnerable position.

4. *The 'touching' question.* Many members of the profession advise teachers never to touch a child, because it can be misinterpreted as an assault. This advice is relatively easy to follow in a secondary school, but in an infant school, small children often want their shoelaces tied, cut knees wiped or a cuddle when they fall and hurt themselves. Unjust as it may seem, statistically men are more at risk of accusations if they touch a child than are women.

Before you start your teaching practice, it is wise to read the school's policy for dealing with accusations. It is wise to look at its policy for interacting with children because it is easier for the school to defend you if you have stuck to their system. It is better to leave first aid to the school's staff designated for the purpose, tie up shoelaces and buttons only in front of witnesses, and, unless you know the parents well, never to risk giving a distressed child a cuddle. If a child wants to cuddle you, it's often all right to accept the invitation, as long as you do not initiate it or respond to it. If you find it uncomfortable, you can smile and say gently, 'That's very nice, but I don't need a cuddle just now.'

As long as teachers and others working with children are vulnerable to accusations from children, we are stuck with having to take so many steps to protect ourselves.

Relationships with other trainees

Teaching practice can be a lonely business if you find yourself in a school with no other students. Usually, however, there is at least one other student, and it is vital that the students give each other moral support.

This is no time to be competitive. When people at work start competing they stop cooperating – and schools run most efficiently on a basis of unity and teamwork. The same principle applies to students. Sharing and supporting are the keywords. You can discuss your lessons together, offer suggestions and be ready to encourage each other. Tell each other what is going well for you and what mistakes you have made so that they do not fall into the same trap.

Different formats of teaching practice

Teaching practice takes a variety of forms depending on the college or university and whether it is a four-year B.Ed. course or a one-year PGCE.

Teaching practice is tiring but you will benefit by being better prepared for your induction year. There will be a sudden rise in your workload.

Sometimes students find themselves spending a whole hour preparing for a one-hour lesson. This is obviously unsustainable in the long term but in the short term it may be necessary. Try not to look on it as time wasted because the better you are prepared, the better your lesson will be and the experience and any resources you have prepared for it are things that you will take away with you and use in the future.

The B.Ed. course

In some of the B.Ed. courses you can be sent to a school for about four to six weeks, or longer as the years progress. In a primary school the weeks will be divided into two so that you can spend about half in each of two different classes, usually a Key Stage 1 class and a Key Stage 2 class. This is useful because it gives you a modicum of experience of both and helps you make up your mind which you want to specialize in.

A few of the difficulties to be overcome

In a B.Ed. course the teaching practices are shorter, and although this means it is not so tiring, it also means that it is harder to make your mark in a school because you have only just got to know the place by the time the practice is over. Also, the children know that you will be there only for a short period of time. In some schools this makes little difference, but in a school that has suffered high staff turnover it is harder to get the pupils to take you seriously when they know you are here today and gone next month.

If you are doing a school-based course like GTP, you will be there for longer periods and the pupils will probably view you as a member of staff. This makes it easier to get to know the pupils and build up that all-important relationship with them.

Different schools have a different ethos. Something that is valued in one school may be given little attention in another, and so you have to be flexible and ready to adjust to the school. Remember that no school is ever going to adjust to a student.

Getting acceptance from teachers is important. They can be so busy that they find it hard to give you time, so it is you who have to make the extra effort to get on with them, in order to get help from them.

In some schools you will have more freedom to teach what you want than in others. Schools have to teach the National Curriculum, and many will have their schemes of work in place and will probably want you to follow them. They may even have the lessons planned out in detail. This is a large advantage because it gives you a good starting point. You will probably pick up new ideas from them, but you may also want to try out different methods. Some schools are more flexible than others. If you want to change how you deliver the lessons, one way is to accept the school's advice to begin with and then, when you are reasonably well accepted, start making your suggestions. If you have an alternative that is interesting and effective, teachers are more likely to give you a freer hand.

Try to be tactful. I have known students to irritate teachers by being too assertive early on in the placement. A comment like, 'It's great having you give me the lesson plans to make it easier for me but I feel I must try to do more for myself, rather than lean on your expertise all the time. Would it be all right if I planned the next lesson and, if you think it's OK, try it out?' will earn you more licence and is more likely to keep their support and goodwill than a direct argument about the best way to organize the lesson.

Also, it is best to keep at the back of your mind the fact that the school is doing you and your college a favour by helping you to learn, so try not to spoil your college's relationship with the school.

Some teachers do not want to let go of their form and hand over to a student. This is not just possessiveness; students sometimes let a class get out of control and the standards slip. As it becomes clear to them that you can cope, they will gradually trust you more and give you more responsibility – and the more conscientiously and competently you work, the more licence you will have.

Postgraduate courses

In some postgraduate courses you can start by going to a school for two days per week and college three days during the first term. It is great to get down to the job quickly with hands-on experience because there is a lot to learn in less than a year. However, some students have told me that it was difficult to keep their university work and their school work going at the same time. Also, after they took lessons for two days they had to return to college and so they lost the continuity of the scheme of work. Students also find it difficult to establish a working relationship with pupils and teachers on this part-time basis.

Although this arrangement is difficult to get used to, it is important to remember that it will last only a short time, and when you qualify, the problem will disappear, so it is best not to let it worry you now. As the PGCE year progresses, you will be sent to other schools for up to about ten weeks full time, during which you will have to cope with about 60 per cent of a regular teacher's timetable. You will find this more satisfying as you will have the opportunity to build up relationships with pupils and staff and, hopefully, see progress, which is what is so satisfying about teaching.

Easing yourself into the school

This is not advice on the technicalities of organizing a successful lesson. You will receive plenty of that from your lecturers. The following points can apply to anyone.

Which school?

Some lecturers have told me that their colleges are conscientious about matching students to a school where they can do the work that interests them most.

For a successful teaching practice it is essential for students to work harmoniously with their mentor in school. Over a space of time, lecturers build up relationships with the mentors in schools and try to put students into schools where they will have a mentor with whom they can work harmoniously. This of course is the ideal, but even with the best will in the world it is impossible for them to be able to do so in every case. It may not be so easy in a college where the staff have not had the chance to build up enough contacts or become familiar with the staff of all the schools with which they work.

A few tips

◆ If you have any choice in the matter, never go on a teaching practice in a school where a member of your family works. If you make a mess of something, you don't want to have to fight the flak on the home front as well as work. College lecturers are usually sympathetic about organizing this.

◆ If you are allowed any say in where you go, find out from friends and any teachers you know in the town which schools are reasonably satisfying places in which to work.

◆ Before you ask for any particular school, look around the area first.

◆ Look at the school's website for information about the school and in particular look up www.ofsted.gov.uk to read its last inspection report and check its place in the league tables. The more you know about the school, the better.

◆ If you have any definite needs, such as those arising from having children of your own at school, impress on the lecturers early the need for you to be in a school close to home. Most are accommodating about this.

Coping with a range of people

Personal skills are important for teachers and students. Everyone in the school must work in a mutually supportive manner. You are unlikely to succeed unless you can work comfortably with the full range of people.

The following points should help you to deal with each one.

The class teacher or head of department

Within the school the class teacher (primary) or head of department (secondary) is the person on whom you are most dependent, and he or she is the one who writes the report on your performance.

- Try to stay on the right side of the class teacher or head of department. Stay cheerful and offer to help them with extra tasks in the class or department. They can make your job much easier or more difficult.

- Find out the time when your class teacher arrives and try to be in the classroom at the same time or earlier. It is easier for a teacher to be positive towards you when you show you are keen.

- Always ask about anything you don't know. No one will think you foolish; in fact, they will like your willingness to learn.

- If you find yourself working with a teacher or head of department who is unhelpful, make sure that your college supervisor is aware of it.

- If the teacher keeps wandering off and leaving you to cope alone, try not to complain unless it is a very challenging school because it might make you look weak. If you can cope alone, think of it as an advantage because it will give you confidence. Sometimes it is easier to cope without the scrutiny of a teacher's critical eye. Remember that class teachers cannot write a negative report on you if they have not seen your faux pas. If you really cannot manage, just ask the teacher to stay in for the whole of the lesson.

- If the class teacher or head of department tries to press extra responsibilities onto you, tread carefully. If you don't think you can cope, say something tactful like, 'I don't think I can manage that on my own, but I don't mind giving you a hand with it.'

- If a parents' evening takes place while you are there, ask the teacher with whom you have the best relationship whether you can sit in on the interviews. He or she may not allow you to, but if you are allowed to observe the interviews, it is a useful opportunity to pick up a few tips on how to carry out this tricky part of the job.

- If an Ofsted inspection is taking place during your placement, teachers will be taken up with that for the week and perhaps have less time for you. There is no need for you to worry, because the inspectors will be looking more closely at how the senior management team supports its students rather than scrutinizing you.

The pupils

◆ Before you go in, ask the teacher or head of department to explain the discipline strategies used. If you are left alone with a class that is difficult to control, it makes it easier to cope if you use the system to which the children are already accustomed. Consistency is the keyword.

◆ Ask the teacher whether there are any pupils' personal circumstances you should know about, for example a bereavement, or parents separating.

◆ Get a friend to go through your hair to check for nits. If you catch them, they can be removed with a fine-tooth comb, or ask at the chemist for a special shampoo for the purpose. In fact, get a fine-tooth comb anyway because during recent decades there have been epidemics of nits. This is not just a problem in impoverished inner-city schools; it can happen anywhere. If you have long hair, they are more easily avoided by wearing it up.

◆ Be wary of the advice about stimulating the pupils all the time. It makes them hyper-excited. Always throw in a peaceful lesson each day.

Your college supervisor

◆ Always make your supervisors welcome when they come in to observe your lesson. They are human too and you need to keep them on your side.

◆ If you have the dilemma of your college giving you a list of tasks that the class teacher or head of department refuses to allow you to carry out, it is wiser to accommodate the teacher, who has the power to insist anyway. Explain to your supervisor that you were afraid to press the issue in case it spoiled the college's relationship with the school. I have known students who tried to solve the problem the other way round, and the most miserable weeks of their college careers ensued.

◆ When your college supervisor gives a demonstration lesson, remember to say that it was interesting/stimulating/achieved its objective.

What you can expect of your college supervisor

Your supervisor is there to support you if you feel you are not getting adequate support in school. Some students have been in schools where they were given the worst classes, probably because the over-pressured teachers saw their presence as an opportunity for them to have a break.

If you find yourself in this position, tell your supervisor at once. He or she may be able to persuade the head or head of department to give you a more reasonable timetable.

Supervisors must also keep a close check on the quality of your lessons. Whether your observed lesson goes well or not, it is important that you listen carefully to the detailed feedback. If you are told that some part of the lesson is not adequate, ask for practical guidance to improve it. Remember that it is your supervisor's job to support and guide you.

Also, they can help you accomplish the long, scary list of professional standards. When you meet them, show them which you believe you have achieved and ask their advice on which standard to try next and any suggestions for ways of trying to achieve it.

Your mentor

Your mentor is a teacher in the school who is there to guide, support and advise you throughout the teaching practice. For you, he or she is probably the most important person in the school, so it is vital to cultivate a positive relationship with your mentor. In a primary school he or she may be one of the class teachers in whose class you are working; in a secondary school the mentor may be the head of department.

Many mentors are excellent, on top of the job, ten steps ahead of you and can give you exactly the right pointers to put you right and give you reassurance when things do not go well. Others are under so much pressure from inside and outside the school that the student on teaching practice is a low priority.

Your mentor's first impressions of you in the initial two or three weeks will be the ones that will stick and be hardest to change. Throwing yourself into the job right from the start will definitely work to your advantage. You also need to bear in mind that no two schools are exactly alike and that the ethos of one can be totally different from that of another even if they are in the same neighbourhood. Your mentor is there to tell you what is accepted practice and what is frowned upon.

It will be easier to start off on the right foot if you ask your mentor about the following:

◆ *The behaviour policy*. Discipline is far easier to maintain if everyone in the school is following the same code of practice.
◆ *Books, stock, equipment procedure*. I am referring here to practical

everyday issues such as whether you can help yourself in the stockroom or whether there is a book to sign and a list of goods to be recorded. Ask to see what equipment is available for your subject(s) and where it is kept. If the stockrooms are kept locked, only senior staff allowed in and stock is dispensed once a day or week, then tread carefully, because this is often a sign that the staff are shown little trust.

◆ *Being there.* Find out whether you are expected to attend staff meetings and make a note of the dates in your diary because it is embarrassing if you miss them. You will probably be expected to attend school assemblies. You should go to them all because the staff are normally expected to attend, and it irritates them if you are seen to be skiving. It is also an opportunity to pick up a few ideas for the future.

◆ *Staffroom customs.* Find out whom you have to pay for tea, coffee and lunches, and pay up-front. In a few schools, teachers are quick to notice things like this. I once worked in a school where you were allowed a full cup or half a mug of coffee, not a full mug; and another where you were not allowed a teabag to yourself; you had to share with a colleague.

◆ *The staff dress code.* It causes resentment if you do not adhere to it.

The rest of the staff

◆ Offer to do playtime duties. That will balance out a few faux pas.

◆ If there is an educational or fund-raising event in an evening or at a weekend, it is worth your while turning up to help. That will obliterate all your faux pas.

◆ If you take pride in your honest, forthright manner of speaking, curb your style for a few weeks. I have known students to have a miserable teaching practice after irritating everyone by giving them the benefit of their advice on how to improve the school.

◆ Never allow yourself to be drawn into the staffroom politics. It takes longer than the duration of a teaching practice to work out the structure of it, and it is never worth the grief.

◆ If your mentor or another teacher invites you to join the staff in the pub, it is well worth going because it helps to build up a relationship with them and it all makes it easier to keep the wheels turning.

Staying sane

◆ When you feel like giving up, remember that the teaching practice is temporary and you are there to learn for your own benefit.

Remind yourself that it will be completely different when you have your own class(es), and keep going.

◆ Stay in close touch with friends from college. You can all share your troubles and comfort each other.

◆ If you are allowed a few days off for illness during teaching practice, do try to resist the temptation to take a sickie if things become difficult. Remember, you might actually be ill later on, and you will end up having to do extra teaching practice during college holidays if you have had too much time off.

◆ You will be amazed how time-consuming the work is, but try to find a period in the week to do something entirely different. A change is as beneficial as a rest.

◆ If you are cooped up in a centrally heated building all day, it is worthwhile taking a walk outside at playtime or lunch time to get some fresh air. This is time well spent as it makes you more alert in class.

◆ Eat a nutritious lunch and try to find a period at lunch time when you can sit quietly on your own and unwind if you have had a stressful morning. If you are able to relax, it will enhance your performance in the afternoon.

◆ Teaching practice is tiring. You may find you need extra sleep. Worse − you will probably have to curb your social life. Many students resent this but it is worth it for a few weeks and much better than failing and having to do an extra placement.

◆ When the practice is over, round up a bunch of friends and go out for the night to celebrate or drown your sorrows. It won't improve your grade or report, but it will cheer you up if things have gone wrong.

When you are starting to find your feet

The importance of feedback

After the first few weeks, ask your mentor for feedback if you have not already had it. Ask the mentor to be specific about what you should focus on to come up to standard. Tell him or her, 'I want to improve on these things so that when I want to apply for a job, I can't be told that I was not up to standard.' Make it clear that you are eager to get things right as you will need all the skills the following year.

You need to make the effort to make your mentor work with you. Honesty is very important in your relationship with your mentor. If you are not doing what you are meant to be doing, it is important that your mentor keeps you informed. It is also important that he or she gives you the hard facts when necessary. Make it clear that you need the absolute truth from your mentor even if it is negative.

Monitoring your own progress

At your weekly meeting with your mentor, as with your college supervisor, it is sensible to bring your list of professional standards, which you will have received from your lecturers. This list looks quite daunting at first as there are a great many targets that you have to achieve.

Show them which you believe you have achieved in the previous week and ask them to sign your file if they agree. Ask their advice on which you should try next and how you might go about it. There are so many to get through that it is important to try a couple each week as it could be hard going if you leave them all to the end. See Part 3 of this chapter, on professional standards, for suggestions.

If you are on a postgraduate course, at the end of the first term ask again whether your improvement has been enough to bring you up to standard, and do the same after the first few weeks and at the end of term in your second school. Unless your mentor has given you specific issues over which you are underachieving, it is difficult for him or her to fail you.

Getting the support you need

If the mentor is not giving you the support you need, then this really must be tackled – with the mentor him- or herself in the first instance. It is unfair to go to the coordinator of the mentors before speaking to the mentor first. If this does not work, then speak to the coordinator, and after that your college supervisor if speaking to the coordinator does not work. At all costs avoid confrontation and do not antagonize them: it is they who will pass or fail you, and they have the biggest input into judging your ability to be a teacher. Try a line like, 'I know you have a lot on at the moment but I would be really grateful if you could help me/give me some guidance on . . .'

When you finally apply for a job, the head will seek a reference from your mentor, so on your final placement it is especially important to build up a successful relationship.

And now to the business of the job.

Getting ready to teach lessons

Before you have to do any teaching yourself, you will have an opportunity to sit in a classroom to observe the teacher and get a feel for the class. It may also be an opportunity to collect information needed for carrying out some assignments.

Always keep a notepad handy to jot down anything that you might find useful for the future.

It is worth taking the following precautions to smooth the way:

1. *Establish the ground rules.* Before you go in, chat to the teacher about what, how and where the teacher wants you to be. Some teachers are very easygoing and allow you complete freedom to wander around the room, look at children's books and join in helping them with the work set. Some will even say that you are welcome to chip in and add anything you wish, if it is a subject at which you are proficient.

   However, even experienced and successful teachers are self-conscious about being observed and may prefer you to sit silently and unobtrusively at the back. Therefore, it is important to get things clear to avoid causing difficulties later.

2. *It is too soon to be assertive!* It is important to go along with the teacher's wishes, at least until he or she gets used to you. If a conflict arises, remember that in all probability the head will back the teacher against you.

3. *Beginning to establish a relationship with the pupils.* When the teacher allows you to get involved, you can start asking the pupils what they are doing and show them that although the class is under the control of the teacher, you are eager to be involved as well, and let them see that you are interested in their work. You can start by asking questions to test their understanding of the work or asking a question designed to extend what they have learned. Let them see that you can teach them. If they feel they can learn from you, they will give you more attention than if you have sat on the sidelines, in their eyes doing nothing.

   Don't be afraid of questions about being a student teacher. It doesn't matter if they know you are not yet qualified. Children and teenagers are quite nosy. They will probably ask you about your accent and where you come from if it is different from theirs.

   However, some might start asking how old you are and whether you have a girlfriend/boyfriend. Such questions can be fended off politely with an answer like 'Oh, that's my little secret.'

It's never wise to get too pally. Children expect teachers to be teachers, not one of their mates.

Observing lessons

Observing lessons has a twofold purpose:

Carrying out assignments
The dynamics of the classroom is a complex business. There are many things happening in the classroom that an untrained eye will not spot. Students are given a series of tasks focusing on different themes such as relationships between pupils and teacher, behaviour management techniques or styles of teaching.

Learning about handling lessons
You need to learn as much as you can about controlling pupils, and stimulating them to learn. Look at the following issues:

◆ The use of questioning:
  – What sorts of questions does the teacher ask?
  – Can questions be answered with a simple yes or no, or do the pupils have to give an explanation?
  – Does the teacher just ask for information or does he or she stimulate the pupils' thinking?
  – Do the questions test understanding?
  – Are the questions random or are they structured to become a little bit more complicated each time?
  – How does the teacher distribute questions?
  – Do the pupils always give their answer straight to the teacher, or does the teacher have the pupils explain their answer to their partner first?
◆ The organizing and managing of a vast amount of equipment for a practical subject such as art or science.
◆ Organizing and coping with large classes when the lesson involves a lot of pupils moving round the classroom and using a lot of equipment to carry out a variety of tasks.
◆ Provision for a wide range of abilities.
◆ Techniques for managing pupils' behaviour.

If all of the above are too much to take in at once, at the beginning just concentrate on one of these issues per lesson.

Lecturers say that students are given a variety of observation tasks, one at a time, so that they can build up an increasingly wide view of classroom practice. As the days progress, you will find yourself trying to carry an ever-increasing load of information in your head, so it is important to make the load lighter for yourself by carrying a pen and notepad.

Alternatively, if you had a very confident teacher to observe, you could ask whether you could video a lesson. You might be lucky enough to be allowed to do so.

Learning how to deliver lessons

When the assignments are finished, you then have to learn to deliver lessons satisfactorily. It is important to be aware of the objective of each lesson and understand how the lesson is structured to achieve it. Always ask the teacher for a lesson plan, so that you can follow the lesson as it progresses.

Many lessons are in three parts, with a starter, main part and plenary to pull the main parts of the lesson together and test whether the objective has been achieved. Watch how one part of the lesson flows into the next part.

The quality of teaching and learning

Look out for these points; they help you decide what creates a successful lesson and give you an idea of the type of teacher you want to become:

- Does the teacher state the objective at the beginning and make sure the children understand it?
- Are the pupils interested and enjoying their work; are they on task and involved in the learning activities?
- How is the lesson organized? Is the teacher doing all the work and the pupils sitting passively? Or are they working independently, or cooperatively in groups? Or is there a mixture of these?
- Does the teacher do all the telling and explaining or are the pupils given tasks that guide them to find things out for themselves?
- Which of the above do they do more willingly? Which is more productive?
- How does the teacher coax the less interested pupils to take part?
- How does the teacher deal with the pupil who is hell-bent on disrupting the lesson?
- Is there much interaction between the teacher and pupils, and

between pupils and other pupils? What effect does this interaction have on learning?

◆ Does the teacher return to the objective of the lesson to check whether he or she has achieved it? Have the pupils grasped the concept or developed the skill, or do they understand the information that was the point of the lesson?

◆ At the end, do the pupils look as though they have gained some knowledge, skill or satisfaction from it or been bored and irritated by it?

As well as concentrating on how the teacher delivers the lesson, you might like to consider some of the issues below. There are too many suggestions to consider in one go; you might choose one at a time. Remember that keeping pupils under control, interested and learning satisfactorily is a complex business and one that takes time to perfect. You cannot expect to get it all right at first.

The hidden curriculum
The hidden curriculum is not to be found in any National Curriculum document, but many teachers, including me, believe it is central to the success of every school. It is the set of rules of behaviour by which the staff and pupils conduct themselves. Qualities of kindness, honesty, respect for other people, property and authority all set the tone of the school and are the foundation of a happy, successful school, one that pupils want to attend and teachers want to work in.

I have always found that the general ethos of a school and the behaviour and interpersonal relationships of the staff and pupils reflect the personality of the head. Those heads who treat the staff even-handedly and with appreciation tend to have a staffroom full of people who extend the same goodwill to their colleagues and pupils.

You may have come across the term 'hidden curriculum' in college. Teaching practice provides an opportunity to put the theory into practice. Observe the teachers and how they conduct their relationships, and of course make a note of those points that promote harmony and cooperation.

You can get a fair idea of the school's hidden curriculum by observing these points:

◆ Is the atmosphere calm, strained, pressurized, happy, hostile? Is there a sense of well-being?
◆ What does the teacher do to influence the atmosphere?

- Listen to the classroom noise. Is it a hum of activity caused by positive effort to accomplish a task? Is it an argumentative, aggressive noise directing pupils' attention away from their work?
- How would you describe the teacher–pupil relationship? Is it friendly, respectful, cooperative, antagonistic, hostile?
- Is the classroom a pleasant environment for teaching and learning? Do the wall displays contain interesting examples of children's work? Are they informative, attractive, inspiring, or, alternatively, boring, faded from being there too long or falling off the walls?

Behaviour management

Before you start, it is a good idea to read the school's policy on behaviour management, because pupils are more likely to respond positively to you if you use the set of rules with which they are familiar. Management of pupils is crucial to delivering the curriculum successfully, keeping the pupils on board and preserving the teachers' sanity.

Depending on how the pupils are normally managed and the level of support that the parents give to the teachers, it can be an easy, straightforward task or a horrendously difficult one. These points give a few clues as to how well it is done:

- How long does it take the class to settle down after break-times or first thing in the morning? A minute, 5 minutes, 10 minutes?
- How much time is wasted through the pupils coming in late, the teacher arriving late, resources not being readily to hand, misbehaviour of pupils or conflict between pupils or teacher and pupils?
- How does the teacher control the pupils? Does he or she instil fear, use incentives, rewards, punishments, or a mixture of some of these, and which does he or she use most?
- How does the teacher deal with difficulties? Does he or she anticipate them and prevent them happening?
- Does classroom layout play a part in managing behaviour?
- Does the teacher's relationship with the pupils play any part in how well he or she controls them?
- Do the pupils automatically give their allegiance to the teacher or does it have to be earned?

Establishing satisfactory behaviour management

If several teachers in the school have difficulty with a particular class, then that is not a suitable class for the novice teacher. Sometimes teachers exhausted by disruptive classes see the student as a resource to give them a break. You could diplomatically ask your mentor or your supervisor to support you by asking that you be given a different class. Don't worry that you might look weak. Their job is to give you positive experiences from which you can learn. They must ensure that students do not have to cope with too much too soon, so that they give up and the profession loses them.

If you cannot escape from having to take the ultra-challenging class, at least don't demoralize yourself by thinking their behaviour is your fault. Comfort yourself with the thought that teaching practice is short and you will then escape.

Behaviour management can be made easy for you from the start if the regular class teacher is in the classroom with you to back you up. Also, pupils are less likely to misbehave if their teacher is watching. But, of course, eventually you will have to learn to cope alone.

Establishing a positive relationship with pupils is the foundation of effective behaviour management. If you start off well, the rest falls into place more easily. If you and the pupils rub each other up the wrong way on the first lesson, it can take a long time to mend the situation, probably longer than the duration of your placement.

Keep it at the front of your mind that all children and teenagers have an overwhelming need to be acknowledged and valued as people, especially the ones who appear hostile or indifferent. If you can get across to them the feeling that you consider them and their education to be important, they will be far more amenable.

Try to learn the pupils' names as soon as you can and try to pronounce unfamiliar names correctly. Some children (and adults) are offended by hearing their names pronounced wrongly and it is easier to get their attention if you address them correctly.

Suggestions for learning names quickly

◆ You can play an alliterative name game to start. The first person introduces him- or herself by adding something they like, using the first letter of their first name – for example, 'My name is Meera and I like making muffins.' The second might say, 'My name is Frank and I like football.' After every sixth person, stop them to give yourself a chance to say their names. When you think you know them all, tell them to change places to see whether you can still name them all.

An alternative name game is to ask the first pupil to say his or her name and the second to introduce him- or herself and the first as well; the pupils in turn introduce themselves and each one before them. For example:

– My name is Abdul.
– My name is James and this is Abdul.
– My name is Chloe, this is James and this is Abdul.
– My name is Tilly and these are Chloe, James and Abdul.

After about every sixth pupil, enter into the chain yourself and try to recall all the names. This one works for me.

◆ Seat the pupils in register order until you know all their names. This is effective in secondary schools where you have to learn the names of a few different classes.

◆ When calling the register, take a few seconds after each name to look at the pupil to memorize their appearance.

◆ Give pupils a piece of scrap paper creased in half and ask them to write their name on it, and stand it up on the desk in front of them so that you can read it.

◆ Each time you speak to a pupil, try to use their name, to fix it in your memory.

Ground rules

Most of the following tips can apply to teaching in either primary or secondary schools.

◆ Start each lesson on time; set the tone that the pupils have to be present and prepared at the start of each lesson. This is especially important in secondary schools, where the school's students are changing class and have every opportunity to be late.

◆ Speak respectfully to pupils. You will only get respect if you give it out. Use a quiet, firm, polite manner to lay down your parameters before you start.

◆ As far as possible, use the same discipline strategies for incentives and rewards as those used by their regular teacher. The pupils respond better when the routine is clear and consistent.

◆ Make it clear in advance what you want pupils to bring to each lesson.

◆ If you know in advance that a pupil is likely to be tricky, it is a good idea to ask a teacher who teaches him or her what works best.

◆ Alternatively, catch out the difficult pupil doing the right thing.

When they are doing what you want, say, 'That's cool, Simena.' Doing so is much more effective than rebuking the pupil for doing the wrong thing.

◆ Establish a clear, simple routine to your lessons at the beginning. When you are feeling more confident that your pupils are under your control, you can try more adventurous lessons.

◆ Always prepare much more work than they can handle. The devil soon finds work for idle pupils.

The 'do' list

◆ Try to stick to the school behaviour policy as consistently as you can. Pupils like to know where they stand.

◆ Always give a clear explanation if there is a change of procedure. No one likes to be confused.

◆ Listen to pupils. They love it, especially the worst-behaved ones. Often they don't have enough opportunity for conversation at home.

◆ Have a system for attracting everyone's attention. Some infant teachers rattle a tambourine. For older children, I always say, 'Hands up those who are listening,' and follow it up by adding, 'Good, Abdul, you can go out at playtime,' to whoever's hand goes up first. In a secondary school, raise your voice a little and say, 'Quiet, please. Quiet, everyone. Third time, quiet!' Another effective approach is always to establish the practice of releasing first, at the end of the session, the pupils who were giving their attention.

◆ If a child is messing about when he or she should be working, start with 'Can you manage? Would you like some help?' Not 'Stop talking/stop messing about/don't be so lazy.'

◆ When you get comments like 'I'm not doing this, I don't want to,' smile sweetly and say, 'No problem, you can do it at lunch time.' Or, 'That's fine. You can take it home and do it. I'll speak to your parents and tell them. They won't mind' — whichever succeeds best with the individual child. This often works, especially after you have carried it out a time or two.

◆ Alternatively, if you think the pupil can't rather than won't do the work, say, 'It's all right, I'll come and help you. Which part are you finding difficult?'

◆ Remember, pupils who don't respond to threats and sanctions often respond to praise. Use lots of it on disruptive pupils, when you can.

- Give positive instructions: 'Please work quietly,' not 'Stop making that din.' Or, 'Write slowly and carefully to keep it neat,' not 'Stop rushing through it and making a scruffy mess.'
- Before imposing a sanction, give pupils a clear chance to conform. You might say, 'Your behaviour is not acceptable; you have got from now to lunch time to get yourself back on track or your lunch break will be spent in here working with me.' Or establish a practice of three strikes and you're out. That is, each time you give a warning, remind the pupil that if he or she has to be warned twice/once more, he or she will be in detention, lose break-time or whatever is the normal practice.
- Always try to impose sanctions the same day if at all possible. They lose their effectiveness if they drag into the next day.
- Once you have made the threat and the pupil is determined not to conform, make sure you carry it out. Pupils will never take you seriously again if you don't.
- Seating arrangements can alter pupils' behaviour. Seating boys beside girls sometimes calms either one of them down, or you could seat hard-working pupils beside those not so desperate to learn.
- Try to come across as one who is there to help them and so it becomes unreasonable for them to try to undermine you.
- Keep the praise flowing, but not so much that you devalue it.
- Ask another teacher whether you can observe him or her working with the class so that you can see how that teacher manages the behaviour. Observation is one of the best ways of learning.
- Keep notes about any serious incidents in case there is any problem with parents later.
- If a pupil is cheeky, never ignore it or give the pupil the satisfaction of seeing that it winds you up. You might reply, coldly but calmly, 'Rudeness will never get you anywhere with me. If you do not know how to speak to other people politely, I can keep you here at break-time and teach you.'
- We all love rewards. Establish an incentive scheme if a class is particularly difficult. Put up a chart with all the names down the side and give points in the form of stickers, or smiley faces on the chart for effort, good behaviour, kindness to others etc. Offer a small reward such as a certificate you have made on the computer, extra computer time, or a small prize from the pound shop.
- Alternatively, divide the class into teams and put up a chart with the teams' names and give a reward of a sticker for their team with

a small extra reward for the best team at the end of the week or month, or at half-term.

◆ Make some praise cards on the computer. They are about six centimetres square, with a fancy border from Border Art or a picture from clip art saying things like 'Good listener', 'A great pal', 'A hard worker', 'Kind to others', 'Super maths brain'. Laminate them and, when appropriate, give one to a pupil who has shown an improved effort or attitude. Let the pupil keep it on his or her desk for the rest of the day (primary) or rest of the lesson (secondary).

◆ In a primary school, when a child has done something well, say, 'That's fabulous, you're a star,' and sprinkle a pinch of glitter on their hair. They love it.

The 'don't' list

◆ Never actually lose your temper. If you lose control of yourself, you have almost certainly lost control of them. In the more challenging schools, pupils love to see a teacher losing it while they sit back and grin. You can, of course, have a controlled loss of temper – that is, just pretend to have lost it. This can work if you do it on rare occasions only.

◆ Never back a child into a corner from which the child cannot escape, otherwise he or she will come out fighting. Try always to give the child an opportunity to get out of a tight corner and conform.

◆ Never keep on repeating the same punishments which are clearly not working. If a sanction (or a reward) does not work after two or three attempts, try something different.

◆ When pupils threaten to bring their parents to the school to sort you out on their behalf, don't look dismayed. Lift your diary and say, 'That's great, I was hoping to meet them. I'm free this afternoon, bring them in.' I have never known a parent to turn up after that.

◆ Try not to shout at pupils for misbehaviour. (Well, hardly ever.) Noisy teachers have noisy classes. Shouting has more effect the less often you do it.

◆ Never shout to attract attention from a noisy class.

◆ Try not to automatically blame the pupil. He or she may well be at fault, but sometimes pupils are insecure in the presence of new teachers, particularly if they have an unstable home. It may be that they are preoccupied with home problems and your lesson is the least of their worries. Don't be afraid to ask your mentor or a class teacher for advice. They know the pupils and their background and the reasons for their behaviour, and often a few quiet tips can reduce the problem.

◆ If a child is cheeky and you respond in the manner of a teacher who has been there for 20 years – the 'I have never in all my life heard such nonsense ...' sort of comment – the children will know you are bluffing and it will make them eager to expose you. You could say, 'I used to try that one with students when I was at school. It didn't work then and it won't work now.'

◆ Never try to be one of the lads/gals. It will backfire because they will not take you seriously as a teacher.

◆ Never let your exasperation show. Save that for your mentor or other students in the staffroom.

◆ Never imagine that you know it all. I have been teaching for 34 years and am still learning new strategies. If you make mistakes, be prepared to learn from them.

For a huge range of interesting and practical ideas, read *Getting the Buggers to Behave* by Sue Cowley. It is a user-friendly book written in a conversational style and should be on every teacher training reading list.

Other adults in the classroom

It is not enough to sort out the curriculum and the pupils. As the job has become more complex and its demands increase annually, it has become the accepted practice to have more adults, qualified and unqualified, in the classroom. A few teachers prefer to work solo, but many are efficient at using the help of others to benefit the pupils. Consider the following:

◆ What other adults are working in the classroom – classroom assistant, parent volunteer, support teacher, advisory teacher?

◆ What are their roles and how do they contribute to the children's learning?

◆ Do the other adults work in isolation with their own little group at an activity that is different from what the rest of the class are doing, or do their pupils take part in the same lesson as the class with the help of the adult? Does the other adult share the lesson delivery equally with the class teacher?

◆ What is the difference between the role of a qualified person and that of an unqualified person such as a parent volunteer?

When you have observed several teachers, you might like to reflect on these points:

◆ Does the 'hidden curriculum' vary from one class to another?
◆ Do the teachers all manage their children's behaviour in the same way? How do they vary? Do different techniques provide different types of behaviour?
◆ What prompts the difference in their methods? Is it the age of the pupils, the number of disruptive pupils in the class or the teachers' personality, or a mixture of these?
◆ Do different teachers treat their support staff in the same way or differently?
◆ Which teaching styles inspire the pupils the most and the least?
◆ How does the atmosphere of the classroom affect the quality of learning?

Observing the points above should give you ideas about how you want to organize your lessons when you start teaching.

It is a tall order to get all of the above issues absolutely right in every lesson. It's a bit like driving a car; an experienced, competent driver makes the task look easy. Similarly with teaching; it takes a lot of practice to get to the stage of making a complicated lesson look easy.

Also remember that the process of getting everything right is a never-ending journey. After 30-something years at the chalk face, I am still learning new tricks of behaviour management and providing more interesting ways of engaging pupils in active learning. Don't let difficulties get you down or failed lessons dishearten you. See them as an opportunity to learn something new and improve your performance.

As with the pre-course placement, it is worth taking the time to jot down notes on anything you see that might be useful for the future.

Styles of teaching

In the beginning, with unfamiliar pupils you might like to copy the regular teacher until you find your feet. This is fine for feeling your way in gently and safely. The teacher will appreciate your compliance with his or her advice. When you have gained some confidence, then is the time to experiment. Ultimately you will develop your own style, for there is no need to be a clone of someone else.

When you are on teaching practice, don't be afraid to experiment. If things go wrong, it doesn't really matter, because no one is expecting you to get everything right. On the first teaching practice you might be team-teaching with another PGCE student or class teacher. This makes it easier if the lesson needs a lot of organizing.

Don't be afraid to experiment and take a few risks. This is an opportunity to find out what works and what doesn't. Students and teachers who have never had a failed lesson have probably never tried to do anything more exciting than the bog-standard. Even if the lesson collapses, you will probably learn something from it. Teachers and lecturers should be sympathetic as long as you have put effort into the planning and made a conscientious attempt to get things right.

The following suggestions can be adapted to either primary or secondary schools.

Variety is the spice of life. Routine in our lives is useful to let us all know where we are going, but with teaching it is important to vary the activities because it all becomes very humdrum and unstimulating if there is no element of surprise.

Keeping their attention. It is tempting to imagine that the fact that they are sitting quietly looking at you means they are taking in all you say, but frequently pupils realize that if they sit quietly and say nothing, you will do all the work while they mentally go to sleep. This is talking at pupils and must be avoided because most of what you are saying is going over their heads. Remember that they have limited concentration, like all of us, and their attention will wander if you do not make sure you are talking to them and they are engaging with you.

Use questions to keep everyone's attention.

◆ If you need to give a long or complicated explanation, you can stop every three or four sentences to ask a question to maintain their attention. To engage them all in the answering, ask, 'Will the bulb in this circuit light up? Hands up those who say yes. Hands up those who say no. Hands up those who don't know.' Then ask a pupil to explain why or why not.

◆ Give out small whiteboards and dry-wipe markers, or scrap paper, at the beginning. When you ask a question, ask the pupils to write the answer on the whiteboard and hold it up. They usually like doing so and it forces them all to participate. (This applies particularly to primary classrooms.)

◆ Engage them in the active learning. If a question needs a complicated answer, ask the pupils to turn to their neighbour and take turns in explaining it, before asking someone to explain to the class.

Working in companionship is more fun. Let them occasionally carry out tasks in pairs. Worksheets can look so tedious to work on, on your own. Let them occasionally do them with a partner. They spark ideas off each other and the companionship encourages them. It often works well if one is a little more able than the other, but of course you must not allow the most and the least able to work together because they often irritate each other, as one soon gets left behind. However, it is not advisable for them to work in pairs all the time as they need to be able to work independently as well.

Interactive whiteboards

An interactive whiteboard (IWB) is a computer-operated screen that allows you to interact with the computer. It has a special surface with a laser attachment that enables you to interact with the software by moving images and captions on the board.

Most schools have either SMART Boards or Promethean boards. They are a boon to the modern teacher. Students who have had regular ICT lessons throughout their schooling are often more competent with them than the more experienced teachers in the school. Pupils love them and so you can add a creative touch to your lessons. Of course, you must save all the information in a well-organized system to save time in the future.

Before you start, ask the ICT coordinator to show you the school's software. Also, beware of turning into the sort of teacher who has pupils on the carpet for long periods staring at it every day. On an IWB course that I attended, the trainer warned us not to forget about collaborative group-work, research using books and artefacts, learning through drama. 'Don't give them death by SMART Board!' she added. Excellent advice.

When using the IWB for a class lesson, be wary of asking pupils to go to the SMART Board one at a time to move some words or symbols or to answer a question. In a class of 30, it can be a long wait for your turn, and pupils get bored. Give them out small whiteboards and dry-wipe pens to write answers and hold up the board. This ensures that they all take part. You can let the pupils take turns to sit at the computer to click the correct answers on the keyboard.

If you find an activity such as a maths game where the board has to be tapped lots of times in quick succession, line them up to take turns. It works if it is a fast activity.

Creating your own slides that are tailor-made to suit your lesson is ideal, although time-consuming, so it is important to save them all on hard disk in well-organized and clearly named files, as well as on a disk or memory stick, to be doubly safe.

You can use the IWB as a stimulus for adventure fiction writing. Let the pupils work in groups of twos or threes and ask them to choose a setting – space, the desert, rainforest, Antarctica, a storm at sea. Take one or two digital photos of each group and download them onto the IWB. Strip away the background, leaving just the outline of the children. Decrease the size of the children and put the image onto a background of a rainforest, spaceship or whatever the children have chosen as their setting. I tried it and my pupils were really excited, and it got their creative juices flowing beautifully. You can of course then use the photos to illustrate their neat or typed copies.

There are literally thousands of websites that add an element of creativity and fun to your lessons. Every time I use a website on which the pupils enjoyed the activity, I always copy, paste and print out a copy for each pupil to take home and use. They always appreciate it. These ones make a good starting point:

www.primaryresources.co.uk
www.mathszone.co.uk
www.bbc.co.uk/revisewise
www.bbc.co.uk/skillswise
www.topmarks.co.uk
www.ngfl-cymru.org.uk
http://home.freeuk.net/elloughton13/index.htm

Something can be accessed for most subjects by typing the topic into www.google.com or www.google.co.uk or www.schoolzone.co.uk, which have websites that have been evaluated by teachers.

Students soon become proficient at finding the website they want and making slides of their own. Always ask teachers which websites they find work well with the pupils. Most have a huge bank that they are willing to share. And, of course, when you have found a successful website, press the 'favourites' key to add it to your bank of websites.

Drama to involve all

Drama works well in lessons across the curriculum. Each of the following ideas can be adapted according to the topic you are studying and can be used at either primary or secondary level. It is best to build up a relationship with the class before trying it because control is important during these lessons. Here are some suggestions for trying drama across the curriculum.

Discussion groups in history lessons

Put pupils into groups of four, two to be Anglo-Saxons and two to be twenty-first-century people. Each group has to prepare a dialogue in which they explain their own system of law and order (or whatever you happen to be studying in history) to the other and then discuss the merits of each. Each group then present their prepared dialogue to the rest of the class.

Discussion groups in English lessons

Look at whatever book you are reading at the time and select an issue that causes conflict among the characters. For example, if reading Anne Fine's book *The Chicken Gave It to Me*, the pupils can discuss the issue of putting chickens in overcrowded, confined spaces to maximize egg production, against the merits of keeping a smaller number in the open air.

Or if reading Captain Marryat's book *The Children of the New Forest*, the pupils can be divided up into Cavaliers and Roundheads to discuss the merits of their side in the struggle of the Civil War.

If reading *King Lear*, the pupils could get into opposing groups to debate whether the king was an innocent victim or deserved his fate by provoking his daughters into rebellion by his obvious bias for Cordelia. The pupils can have an open class discussion or go into groups to discuss the matter and present their dialogue to the class.

Discussion groups in modern-language lessons

Arrange pupils in small groups to prepare a short conversation using whatever set of vocabulary they are learning at the time, such as a chat about holidays, exams, football, any sport or topical subject.

Collaborative activities: finding out for yourself

Working in mixed-ability groups on an activity is a great way to learn because children give each other ideas, show each other how to find out things and learn the invaluable skill of working cooperatively. This style of teaching often involves pupils finding out things for themselves.

You must always make sure you have an able child in each group to organize the others, and if there is a pupil who is in the early stages of learning English, try to have another in the group who can interpret. Make it clear that the children with special needs must be included. These ideas can be adapted to whatever you are studying.

Geography

Look at the country you are studying, say Egypt. Give each group a blank map of the world, of Africa and Egypt, and one or two atlases. Give them a list of things to find in the atlases and mark on the maps.

Science

Science lessons at all levels involve group investigations. Even Key Stage 1 pupils can take part in simple finding-out activities. Give pupils, in pairs, a piece of insulated wire, a battery and a bulb and tell them to try to find out how to make the bulb light. Or give each pair a magnet and a piece of paper marked 'Magnetic' or 'Not magnetic' and tell them to go round the classroom to find out and record things that fall into each category. Pupils are stimulated by this because it gives them responsibility, and the pleasure of having found out things for themselves is wonderful.

Maths

Brainteasers make a great mental and oral starter for a lesson for pupils to work out in groups. Maths crosswords work well in pairs or small groups, and children love mathematical games. The catalogues usually have a range of games that teach children a skill and, at the same time, add an element of fun to your lessons.

Preparation

Start small. Don't try to achieve too much in the first few lessons and concentrate on quality rather than packing in lots of activities. Write your lesson plan and then ask the teacher to check it. Remember that it is important to take the children's pace of learning into consideration, and the teacher can advise you on that.

Having your lesson observed

Having your lesson observed can be nerve-racking at first, but try to see it as an opportunity to learn.

The acid test of whether a lesson was successful is whether the objective was achieved. You may not always get a warning about when the lecturer is coming, so it is best not to be caught out skimping the preparation.

Be clear in your mind exactly what points you are trying to teach; write the objective on the board and start by making sure the pupils know what it means. Finish the lesson by asking questions to test whether you have succeeded, and, if you have, tell the pupils they have achieved their objective, and add a few words of appreciation.

Hints to get through lesson observations

If there is to be a support teacher in the room, such as a special educational needs or an English as an additional language teacher, discuss together in advance what you would like them to do and give them your lesson plan as well.

If there is a disruptive child in the class, try to place the pupil in the group with the support teacher, who is more familiar to him or her. If you have made a conscious effort to build up a comfortable working relationship with all staff with whom you have to work, they will be more inclined to help you in circumstances like these.

♦ Always make sure you have a detailed lesson plan ready for the supervisor because, if the lesson fails, at least it shows you put time and care into it, and so it won't look so bad.

♦ Don't worry if you have collywobbles, because most students do, and they usually disappear as soon as you become engrossed in the lesson. It is all right if a lecturer realizes you are nervous because the lecturer was once a student too.

♦ If it is a difficult class, tell the college supervisor in advance what the problems are.

♦ Don't worry if the lesson does fail absolutely; it has happened to everyone.

Guidance from the observer

Make sure the person who observed your lesson gives you detailed feedback. This has the dual purpose of reassuring you about the things that went well and helping you to rectify anything that went wrong.

Don't adopt a defensive attitude. Be willing to learn from the feedback because it is designed to help you in the future. If something was poor, ask the supervisor for ideas on how to improve it for the future. Remember, the supervisor is not an inspector; he or she is there to support you and help you to develop your expertise.

Being a reflective practitioner

Being a reflective practitioner is an essential part of the course and a vital element of being an effective teacher. Students who are eager and ambitious often feel disproportionally dismayed when a lesson unexpectedly turns into a mess. If or when this happens to you, there is no need to let it cloud your horizon for long. No student to my knowledge has ever got through college without an occasional unsuccessful lesson, and you should see it as an opportunity to learn, not as a failure on your part.

Writing the evaluations to your lessons forces you to think about how to improve them for the future.

Whether the lesson has been observed or not, ask yourself what things went well and make a list of them. Perhaps a few of the pupils acquired the concept of it or enjoyed it. Maybe the first part went well and then it fell apart when the activity changed. Keep the successful part at the front of your mind before you start analysing why the lesson was not as successful as you had hoped.

What can go wrong
The following are some of the things that can go wrong:

◆ The resources were not properly organized or there were not enough of them.
◆ The work was not pitched at the right level — that is, it was too hard or too easy.
◆ You were not absolutely sure of all your information.
◆ The lesson was not interesting enough.
◆ The pupils spent too much of the time passively listening and not enough time actively participating.
◆ Ten minutes before the end of the lesson, you ran out of things to do.
◆ You were nervous and the pupils realized it.
◆ You rubbed them up the wrong way by acting over-confidently or coming over too heavy too quickly.

- Your behaviour management was not adequate.
- There was a bunch of awkward pupils who didn't want to work and their main aim was to prevent anyone else working or wreck the class whatever you did.
- The pupils have had so many student teachers and supply teachers that they are no longer interested in listening to outsiders.

Always make a note on the lesson plan to help you get it clear in your head so that you do not repeat the errors. The following points might help.

The lesson plan and resources

- Preparation of resources is essential. If you have a lot of them, with worksheets at differentiated levels, a simple precaution is to have Post-it labels stuck on the top copies to avoid the difficulties that arise from pupils getting the wrong one.
- Always have extra worksheets available, one for yourself, one for anyone observing your lesson, a couple for the children who mess it up and one for your file.
- Always have your lesson plan in your hand. You don't need to memorize it until you are more experienced and confident.
- Prepare an extra activity for each lesson so that you won't run out. It is not a waste of time if it is not used, because you can keep it in your file for future reference.
- Getting the lesson pitched at the right level can be difficult for someone who is unfamiliar with the class. Always ask the regular teacher to check your plans and preparation before you take the lesson.
- Variety is the spice of life. The more interesting the lesson, the less likely the pupils are to look to their peers for amusement.

Discipline

- It is important to hold your head up, look pupils in the eye and speak confidently, but if you overdo it they will not be fooled, especially at secondary level. Try not to be overbearing and definitely never speak in a cutting or sarcastic manner.
- Ask your mentor whether there are any behaviour problems in a class before you take the lesson and ask for tips on how to manage. Some classes need to be handled firmly right from the first minute. In others you need to start with a joke and a laugh to get them on your side and then clamp down later if necessary.

◆ Make sure you know the school's sanctions for misbehaviour. It works best if you are all following the same system.

Your frame of mind
Your frame of mind is more important than you think:

◆ It is impossible to teach for long at the limits of your own knowledge. If you are asked to teach a lesson on something unfamiliar, it will give you more confidence if you read up about it before you get caught out. The hour of your time the night before the lesson is easier to cope with than the uncomfortable hour of regret the following night.
◆ If the class gives grief to every teacher, be assured that their behaviour is not your fault. A small minority of classes never give their respect and allegiance to a teacher until they have established a relationship, and that can take a month in a primary school and much longer in a secondary, where you have pupils for only a few lessons per week.
◆ If you are planning something adventurous and are worried that it might fall apart, it gives you confidence if you also have an easier activity ready in case it all goes wrong. Double the work, I know, but it can give you double the confidence, and the planning can always be kept for the future.

Being a reflective practitioner in the school is important because you need to sort out specific problems immediately. In the beginning it is often too complicated to do it alone. Your mentor, your college supervisor, other teachers and your peers can advise you and guide you in overcoming difficulties and correcting mistakes.

When you return to college
When you return to college, it is still important to reflect on the experiences and share ideas with peers. When students are completely away from the pressures of marking, collecting resources for the next day's lessons and worrying about how to manage the behaviour of the next day's classes, it is easier to assess the positive and negative parts objectively. It is reassuring to realize that others encountered similar challenges. Successful colleges recognize the need for evaluation and give students opportunities to discuss with their peers and lecturers what works well and what must be avoided at all costs.

It is often quite productive for students to bring resources they have used or made to group discussion meetings so as to share their ideas. Teachers do this informally in group staff meetings and INSET meetings. Occasionally teachers become precious about their ideas and resources and do not want to share them. This is poor practice. In the best schools, teachers work in a team, supportively and cooperatively, sharing their skills, using their talents to encourage others and taking pride in playing their part in helping others to improve. Foolish teachers become resentful if others copy their ideas. Sensible teachers take it as a compliment.

It is also important to remember that some methods and practices work well with some classes but can be disastrous with others. For example, depending on how they have been trained in the past, some pupils are able to accept more responsibilities for themselves and can be trusted to carry out investigative tasks sensibly, or conduct themselves around the school unsupervised. Others would see this as a heaven-sent opportunity to go for a smoke in the toilets. The practice must be suitable for the pupils as well as achieving the objective.

If you found some of the placement heavy going, it is reassuring to discover that others had a similar experience. Most students find that the chance to talk to other students about what was successful is a valuable opportunity to pick up ideas and console each other.

When you qualify

Being a reflective practitioner is not just for teaching practice. It is an essential element of being a teacher and it is sensible to cultivate, right from the start, the habit of mentally evaluating each lesson. Of course, when you take up an appointment you do not have to write a detailed evaluation of every lesson, but it is good practice to make a mental note of anything that worked well or didn't. A quick phrase or sentence on the lesson plan to remind you when you do the lesson next year should be enough.

Coping with Ofsted while on teaching practice

'Ofsted' is an acronym for Office for Standards in Education. It sends its inspectors to schools to examine every aspect of school life, from the quality of teaching and the efficiency of senior management to budgeting.

In the past, a missive from Ofsted announcing the arrival of its staff usually resulted in weeks, or even months, of feverish activity by the head and teachers to ensure that all paperwork was up to date, the school looked stunningly attractive, and the most imaginative and enjoyable lessons were prepared to keep the pupils interested and on task, the objectives of the National Curriculum were being achieved, the parents were satisfied, and a host of other issues.

At the time of writing, Ofsted gives only two or three working days' notice. This gives the inspection team a far more realistic view of what the school is normally like and saves the teachers from suffering months of needless anxiety.

A small number of students have to cope with Ofsted while on teaching practice. If you find yourself in this position, you might like to consider the following advice.

The 'do' list

◆ Remember that the inspectors are testing the school management's ability to run the school. Even if they do observe one of your lessons, it is the teachers and management that they are really interested in.

◆ Remember, they may be inspecting the school's efficiency in supporting and mentoring its trainees. The focus is on them, not you.

◆ Go to your mentor if you are nervous and ask whether it is absolutely necessary for you to be inspected. If it is your first teaching practice, you have more chance of avoiding it, but if you are nearly qualified, you have little chance.

◆ Tell your college supervisor that you are under more pressure because of the inspection.

◆ Think positively. If your lessons are judged to be satisfactory or better, it will look impressive on your letter of application for your first post.

◆ Keep at the front of your mind the fact that you will not be there to pick up the pieces when the event is over.

◆ Ask your family or flatmates not to expect much sense out of you until the wretched inspection is over.

◆ Forget the social life until it is after the inspection. You can make up for it when it is finished.

◆ Make sure that every detail of your next day's lessons is prepared before you leave each day.

◆ Get a proper night's sleep.

◆ Eat properly and stop for a rest at break-times.

◆ Stay close by any other students who are in the school. You all need each other for support and encouragement.

◆ When it is over, forget anything that anyone has said or done that has annoyed you. Teachers, like everyone else, are less patient and tolerant when under pressure and you still have to work together – and cooperation can only be achieved in an atmosphere of harmony.

The 'don't' list

◆ Don't panic. Panicking tends to reduce the quality of performance.
◆ Don't expect the school staff to be their usual cheerful selves. Their careers are much more affected by the inspection than yours, and arguments over petty issues sometimes arise when people are under pressure.
◆ Don't take a sickie. This destroys your credibility, as others always suspect absentees of malingering. You will get more sympathy and kudos for turning up, even if your lessons are not brilliant.

Parents' consultation evenings

Conducting a parents' consultation evening (sometimes called an open evening) in a confident, efficient manner is a necessary part of the job if you are to maintain your professional credibility. Teachers get little training for it, and many newly qualified teachers face their first parents' evening with trepidation.

You can learn a lot from observing how teachers conduct the interviews, so if a parents' evening occurs while you are on teaching practice, it is sensible to ask whether you can sit in on the interviews with a teacher to pick up some hints on how to conduct them. Some teachers might veto your presence, but you may be fortunate and find a teacher who welcomes your company.

Sitting in on a teacher's interview

The following points can apply to both primary and secondary schools. Some teachers are so expert at handling tricky situations that they make the job look easy. In time you will see that keeping the parents' support makes your job easier too.

You might want to write down a few details afterwards, but obviously not in front of the parents as that could be quite disconcerting for them and perhaps make them clam up. Of course, if the parents are being rude or aggressive, your writing notes might just make them calm down.

The following are some points to note when you sit in on a parents' evening with the class teacher in control:

◆ How does the teacher greet the parents?
◆ How does the teacher make them feel at ease?
◆ What vocabulary does he or she use to break news of poor exam results, or examples of misbehaviour?
◆ How does he or she use different tones of voice?
◆ How does the teacher cope with parents who are distressed by their children's behaviour or poor performance?
◆ How does he or she diffuse a heated situation?

In case you have to do it alone

As a student you will probably not have to cope with a parents' evening on your own, unless you are doing a long placement in a secondary school and you are the person who has had most contact with the class in your subject in the preceding weeks or months.

Parents' evenings are tiring after a long day at work, but if you do take part in one, the experience will give you some confidence for when you have to do it on your own the following year. The suggestions below are for students who find themselves facing parents alone.

Know the score

In some schools there can be parents who view the open evening as an opportunity to attack the school in general and the teacher in particular. As a precaution, you could take your class list(s) to a teacher who is familiar with the parents and ask him or her to give you a brief rundown of the list to tell you which may be difficult and how best to handle the situation if it becomes tricky. Of course, you must make a few notes because it is hard to keep it all in your head when you are trying to recall so many details about the children as well.

If you are in a challenging school, ask whether there are any parents with whom it is unwise to be alone, in which case you might like to ask a senior member of staff to accompany you or at least patrol the corridor outside your classroom while you leave the door open.

There may be parents who are over-punitive with their children, and it is important to know this in case a pupil suffers an over-harsh punishment because of something you said.

The last two points are not an exaggeration. I have encountered both on more than one occasion.

Look and feel right

Never start an interview immediately after the pupils go home. Give yourself time to have a cup of tea and a snack, freshen up your face, comb your hair, even change your shirt/blouse before the first parents arrive. Remember, the types of parents who come to scrutinize teachers will be doubly keen to size you up if they know you are a student. If you look and feel fresh, you will perform better.

Be prepared

It is too difficult to keep all the information in your head. Make brief notes on each child. They don't have to be detailed as only you will see them. It is irritating afterwards to remember something you forget to say.

Privacy is paramount

It is important that all details remain strictly private; therefore only have one child's parents in the room at any one time unless it is a large room and you can ensure there will be enough space between those you are interviewing and those waiting.

Keep the atmosphere calm

Sometimes parents are nervous before interviews with teachers. As soon as the parents walk through the door, stand up, smile and say, 'Good evening', and introduce yourself. Whatever the quality of your relationship with the pupil, it is best to start by saying something positive about him or her.

Make sure you are the one in control

Always make sure you are the one to start the dialogue. If you intend to say anything negative, have the pupil's books ready to hand in case the parent argues.

It is more persuasive to make your comments in the form of a fact rather than an opinion. It is better to say, 'I have seen your son deliberately distract other pupils during lessons', rather than 'Your son is badly behaved during lessons.' Similarly, 'Your daughter often arrives late for lessons/regularly leaves her homework at home,' rather than 'Your daughter is lazy/careless/indifferent.' Facts are more difficult to dispute than opinions, and giving specific examples adds weight to your comments.

If you know in advance that you will have to say something negative, ask other teachers whether they have the same problem with the pupil. If so, ask their permission to say that the pupil's behaviour is the same in their classes. It is more difficult to argue if two or three teachers say the same thing.

Use honey, not vinegar

Remember, criticizing a pupil can be hitting a parent where it hurts them most, so it pays to be as diplomatic as you can. Saying, 'I like your son, but unfortunately I do find myself having to nag him to stop having private conversations in class, because it spoils the lesson for others,' is more likely to gain their support and goodwill than 'I'm sick of your thoughtless son trying to wreck my lessons,' even though the latter may be closer to the truth.

Don't let a disagreement turn into a confrontation

Most parents approach parents' evenings in a spirit of goodwill, but a tiny minority come looking for a confrontation, and others become confrontational when they cannot handle a teacher's criticism of their child.

As a student, inexperienced and not yet qualified, you should not have to cope with a confrontation, so you can pass the buck with a clear conscience. If you sense one coming, stop the conversation before it arises, making a comment like 'I think it would be best if you discussed this matter more fully with the head/head of department. Would you like me ask him/her to make an appointment to see you?'

If parents become aggressive or raise their voices, look them in the eye and say calmly but authoritatively, 'I am not prepared to conduct this interview in an uncivil atmosphere. If you cannot speak politely, this interview is now over.' If they do not calm down, stand up and open the door. If they refuse to go, leave the room yourself and go to your mentor or head of department or the headteacher to tell them the full facts as soon as you can. They should support you. In fact, they ought to feel rather bad about putting you into the situation in the first place.

This type of incident really should not happen but it is important to know what to do if it does.

Try to finish on a positive note

If parents are unhappy at the end of the interview, try to make them feel that you are still interested in their child by saying something like 'If you are concerned about anything in the future you can make an appointment to come in and see me again. You don't have to wait for another open evening' (unless of course they are the type of parents who want to come and talk to you for an hour after school on a regular basis).

Self-assessment

After the placement is over, it is good to look back over it and think about what you have learned. Think about these issues and make a list under each heading:

◆ *Teaching styles* – what did you learn?
◆ *Behaviour management* – what new strategies did you discover?
◆ *Relationships with other staff* – what have you learned about their roles and how they can support you? How amicably did you work with them and what did you learn about how to get their support?
◆ *Relationships with pupils* – did they enjoy your lessons? Did they look pleased to see you after a few lessons? Did they show enthusiasm for what you were teaching? Did they want to chat to you at playtime or lunch time?
◆ *Lessons which were observed* – how good did the observer judge them to be?
◆ *Your own self-improvement* – how well did you feel you had acted on advice and improved the quality of your lessons during the placement? Did your own evaluations show that you had sound self-judgement?
◆ *What new experience did you have* – taking assembly, going on an educational trip, sorting out a playground conflict at break-times? Has it taught you something useful that you could use again?
◆ *Did you fulfil some of your professional standards?*
◆ *Did you manage to keep your paperwork up to date alongside your teaching?*

If you are able to put in a few positive things under all or most of these headings, then feel encouraged about it. Be careful not to make the mistake that many teachers make – that of seeing only the negative aspect of their work, or feeling frustrated because they did not get everything right.

After you are satisfied that you have made worthwhile progress, you should then look at skills that you still have to develop. Do not think of them as failures, but rather as just parts of the job that you will try to improve on during the next placement. Look closely at the issues that did not give you so much satisfaction and ask yourself how much was your fault. Some disappointments may have been caused by things that were beyond your control. Perhaps your mentor did not have as much time for you as you would have liked, or the pupils may have had too many changes of teacher in the past and so not been very keen to have another. The journey may have tired you out. Comfort yourself with the knowledge that next time it will be in a different school and the same difficulties probably will not arise.

Now ask yourself what you will to aim to improve on, next time. Make a list of about three issues — no more, because it is better to have a manageable number and make a success of them than to try too many and not succeed. Talk to you supervisor in college and tell him or her what you aim to improve on and ask his or her advice. The supervisor should be impressed that you are handling it in a professional manner.

Above all, keep it at the front of your mind that when you qualify and get a job, it will all be different. You will settle into a school routine and have regular support, and the opportunity to practise everything every day, and so you will build up the skills for the job over time. Never feel frustrated that you cannot do everything as well as you want to. I have been teaching for 34 years and am still learning new skills and strategies, and happy to do so.

Getting organized for the future

For a teacher, time management is vital. Every lesson represents your valuable time and energy, so you need to develop strategies for conserving both. It is never too soon to take a trip to the stationer's to equip yourself with a set of ring binders, file dividers, plastic wallets and sticky labels to start collecting your own resources. You may find an online supplier who delivers cheaply in bulk, so you could club together with other students for an order. Buy paper wallets by the gross; you'll be amazed at how quickly you fill them up.

You can invest in a filing cabinet. You don't need a new one; they can be bought cheaply second-hand from office suppliers. Sometimes you can be lucky and buy a load of used suspension folders to put in them, but do check the sizes before you buy, because they can vary more than you might think.

Look at all your plans and resources. Divide them into two piles: 'save it and file it', or 'chuck it'. Have a section for each subject and subdivide it for Year groups or Key Stages. There is no need to limit yourself to your own ideas. If you see a useful worksheet or resource made by a teacher or student, ask for a copy. As long as you are willing to share your resources, they will not mind you using theirs. In fact, most teachers take the view that imitation is the sincerest form of flattery.

As soon as you have taught a lesson, put a copy of the lesson plan, the worksheet, and any other notes concerning DVDs, websites or books and page numbers into a file. Also, store each lesson plan on your computer as well as memory stick or disk. Have your files labelled for each subject and divided up for each topic, so that the next time you come to teach it, perhaps in three years' time, you can retrieve the information quickly.

Remember, there is no value in collecting resources if they are kept in a muddle. The time you will lose in searching for them will cancel out the time you have saved in keeping them.

PART 3: PROFESSIONAL STANDARDS FOR QUALIFIED TEACHER STATUS

Fulfilling the Professional Standards for Qualified Teacher Status is an important, if onerous, part of the course. In order to qualify for QTS it is necessary to fulfil all of the criteria of the professional standards.

On first looking at this list, you might feel rather daunted at the prospect of having to provide evidence that you can satisfy every single one, but remember that many of them are issues that will come up naturally throughout the year. At the time of writing, there are about 40 sections and subsections to be fulfilled and the course lasts about 40 weeks, so if you aim at two per week, you will be finished with plenty of time to spare. Also, you will note that many of the standards overlap with others, so when you fulfil one, look to see whether it helps you with another.

Some of the topics would make an interesting subject for an essay, project or assignment, so you could study the essay topics to see which ones coincide with a professional standard and so use it as an opportunity to kill two birds with one stone. When you meet your mentor or personal tutor, it is worth bringing your list and discussing with them which ones you want to work on that week and run past them your ideas on how to do it. Once you have established that weekly routine, the list will not seem so daunting.

It is important to fulfil as many standards as you can during teaching practice. When you have your weekly meeting with your mentor in school or your college supervisor, always ask which they feel you have fulfilled and check that they can be signed off; and tell them your ideas for trying in the next week. Don't be afraid to ask for suggestions for which ones you should attempt next. If you aim to fulfil two each week, you should easily work your way through them by the time you reach the end of your last teaching practice.

Remember, some of them are ongoing, and so you might have several occasions to revisit them. At all costs, avoid leaving them to the last few weeks as that can result in avoidable stress.

Where the standard requires you to have knowledge or understanding of an issue, it is wise to ask questions about it. Some students fall into the trap of being afraid to ask questions in case it looks as if they do not know enough. This is the wrong attitude, partly because it prevents you from learning, and partly because teachers and lecturers do not expect students to know everything in any case. They interpret your questioning as evidence of your eagerness to learn, not ignorance of a subject. In fact, when students ask advice about how to help pupils, they interpret that as a shift in their focus from themselves to the pupils and see it as progress in their growing confidence and professional skill.

As you work your way through them, try to think long-term. Try to keep at the front of your mind the fact that you are fulfilling the criteria to give you opportunities to learn and become a competent teacher, not just to get through the course.

The rest of the chapter suggests ways of fulfilling each one. Of course this is not a finite list, nor could you possibly carry out everything suggested below.

Most of the suggestions could apply to either the primary or the secondary level.

The professional standards are grouped under three headings:

◆ professional attributes
◆ professional knowledge and understanding
◆ professional skills

Each section is then divided into subsections. The website www.tda.-gov.uk/upload/resources/pdf/q/qts_standards_guidance_2007.pdf gives the full details of each standard, along with that standard's scope and a list of questions that the training providers need to consider when assessing each student. This website is particularly helpful to students as it lists specific issues on which their lecturers will focus when assessing them. It also adds a list of cross references so that students can see where each standard overlaps with another.

The aim of this chapter is to give students some practical ideas of how they can fulfil each standard.

Professional attributes

Relationships with children and young people

Q1 Have high expectations of children and young people including a commitment to ensuring that they can achieve their full educational potential and to establishing fair, respectful, trusting, supportive and constructive relationships with them.

Suggestions for fulfilling Q1

◆ Add to each lesson plan or worksheet a challenge activity to stretch the more able.

◆ Try to find a place in the lesson for pupils to explain their views or attitudes or method of working. Encourage the others to listen respectfully by setting a good example of doing so yourself. Emphasize that there are many views and attitudes on, and methods for, everything, and we need not all agree, but we do need to respect each person's right to their own opinion.

◆ Setting tasks that have to be completed in pairs or groups is good for teaching pupils to work in harmony.

◆ Ask pupils to explain something and then tell them to explain their view to the pupil beside them before discussing it with the class.

◆ Praise pupils generously, particularly the less able.

◆ When correcting pupils' mistakes, point out what they have done well or got right, before pointing out the errors. Finish with a word of encouragement.

◆ When marking pupils' books, start with a general positive comment and then write 'Target:' and add a suggestion that is suitable for helping that pupil to improve his or her work. One pertinent suggestion is better than lots of red ink throughout the work. After the next piece of work, check whether they have taken your advice and praise them if they have done so.

◆ Let them see that you value them as people. Congratulate them on any out-of-school success, or if they have a member of the family in hospital, ask about that person.

Q2 Demonstrate the positive values, attitudes and behaviour they expect from children and young people.

Suggestions for fulfilling Q2

◆ Read the school's policies regarding discipline and anti-bullying.
◆ If you teach a subject where there is an element of danger — science, PE — always read the safety regulations before you start and, obviously, stick to them closely.
◆ Always be punctual for classes, especially after lunch times and playtimes, because it sends out a negative message if you are always the last one into the classroom.
◆ Likewise, if you have to collect a class from the playground after each break, it promotes a poor attitude if you regularly make your class wait longest in the cold (primary).
◆ Try to start classes on time. Don't make the pupils who have arrived punctually wait for the stragglers (secondary).
◆ Encourage pupils to take pleasure in each other's achievements.
◆ Make certain your own manner of address is respectful by giving polite, positive instructions — that is, 'Please work quietly so as not to disturb others,' not 'Shut up!' or 'Stop that racket!' (This one can be impossible to adhere to in all cases because most teachers will eventually meet a class that makes a point of trying their patience beyond any human endurance.)
◆ Don't be aloof. When you meet your pupils in the corridor, smile or nod. If you meet them in the supermarket or the street, look pleased to see them, smile and say, 'Good morning/afternoon.'
◆ Try to mark pupils' books before you return them. If they are not marked, it looks as though you don't consider the work to be important. If ever you don't have the work marked before returning the books, give a reason and an apology. If you don't mark the work each day, you will be amazed at how quickly the quality will fall.
◆ Offer praise and positive reinforcement more liberally than negative comments. Catch reluctant pupils out doing the right thing and praise them, ignoring lesser elements of negative behaviour when you can.
◆ Remember, pupils take their cue from you. Good manners and kindness to other pupils are learned by copying you.
◆ If you have pupils who have English as an additional language (EAL) or special educational needs (SEN), seek advice from the specialist teacher in that area. The teacher will often be so pleased

that you are taking account of the pupils' needs that he or she will be glad to show you how to differentiate the work for them.

◆ When pupils say, 'I can't do this,' reply with a smile, 'Yes, you can. I'll help you.' I sometimes use the expression 'Yes, you can. I've got faith in you.' If you can persuade the pupils to have confidence in themselves, you have pointed them in the right direction to succeed.

◆ Don't shout (or at least, not more often than you can help). It sends out a bad message about the type of behaviour that is acceptable, and noisy teachers have noisy classes.

The following websites can help you with Q1 and Q2:

www.gtce.org.uk
www.ttrb.ac.uk
www.citizEd.info
www.dfes.gov.uk/behaviourandattendance
www.everychildmatters.gov.uk

Frameworks
Q3(a) Be aware of the professional duties of teachers and the statutory framework within which they work.

Suggestions for fulfilling Q3(a)
◆ Read the documents *School Teachers' Pay and Conditions, Raising Standards and Tackling Workload* and *Every Child Matters*.

◆ Read the school's safety policy and, of course, put it into practice, particularly if you go on a school trip.

◆ Read the school's policy for pastoral care and find out who is the designated teacher to whom children at risk should be referred. Remember that any information you are given about pupils must not be passed on to anyone.

◆ If you have a suspicion that a pupil is being abused, tell your mentor at once and the designated teacher who deals with child abuse. If a child tells you anything that must be reported, you must never promise not to tell anyone else. On the other hand, once you have passed the information on, you must respect the confidentiality of it.

Q3(b) Be aware of the policies and practices of the workplace and share in collective responsibility for their implementation.

Suggestions for fulfilling Q3(b)

◆ It takes a long time to be on the ball with everything that is asked of you in this standard – longer than your placement – so as soon as you are in doubt, ask for help. It is always the best practice. Teachers will appreciate your eagerness to learn.

◆ Read the school's policies on behaviour management, anti-bullying, equality, SEN and EAL.

◆ Ask the form teacher for any details of how to cope with individuals with special needs.

◆ Read the school's National Curriculum policy documents regarding your subject(s).

◆ Turn up and help with any fund-raising or pupils' social events such as school discos that take place while you are on teaching practice.

◆ Offer to help with any extra-curricular activities for which you have a skill, such as by helping backstage for drama productions, helping with the Duke of Edinburgh Award scheme, or accompanying teams on away matches.

◆ Volunteer to go on school trips even if they do not involve one of your classes. (Teachers are always looking for extra support for trips. The experience is beneficial and you will probably enjoy it.)

◆ Offer to take assembly and break duty. You will gain from this too, because teachers will appreciate your effort and probably respond by giving you more support, and a better report.

◆ If an emergency arises, be ready to respond. If a child has an accident or an infant is 'lost' on the premises (it happens on rare occasions), be willing to give support where it is needed.

Communicating and working with others

Q4 Communicate effectively with children, young people, colleagues, parents and carers.

Suggestions for fulfilling Q4

◆ Be a good listener to pupils, teachers and parents.

◆ Ask the teacher about the pupils' home backgrounds. Find out their religions, the languages they speak, how many speak English as their second, third or fourth language. Ask how many have parents who do not speak English, and how much support they are able to give to their children's learning. It all helps you to build up a picture of where the children are coming from, and you need to understand their advantages and disadvantages.

◆ Look out for children in care, asylum seekers and refugees. They have often suffered in the past and lack the sort of security that the rest of us can take for granted. Try to show them extra patience, care and encouragement.

◆ It is important to respect the pupils' need for privacy. Everything you know about them is strictly confidential.

◆ Be aware of the school's cultural mixture of races and creeds. You can let it be known by your treatment of the pupils that you respect them all equally.

◆ Ask teachers whether you may attend parents' evenings if they occur during your teaching practice, even if it is only to sit in on the interview because the teacher does not want you to take part.

◆ Make a point of stopping to speak in a friendly manner to parents as you chance to meet them.

◆ If the teachers are writing reports during your placement, ask whether you can be involved. Ask their advice on which information is important and getting the tone right.

◆ It is impossible to know it all. The golden rule is, ask for help.

Q5 Recognise and respect the contribution that colleagues, parents and carers can make to the development and well-being of children and young people and to raising their levels of attainment.

Suggestions for fulfilling Q5

◆ Consult parents or carers for support if you think it appropriate, but before you speak to a parent, ask advice from the regular teacher, in case the parent is difficult. Tell parents politely of any problems, making your comments sound like a request for help, not a complaint. Try to start the conversation with a positive comment like 'Jimmy is good at getting on with others and working well in class, but I'm finding it hard to get him to bring his homework in on time. I should be really grateful if you could check that he has done it every Tuesday night and put it into his bag.'

◆ Finish the conversation by telling them they are welcome to contact you if they have any concerns about their child's education. (Of course, you should not use this line with parents who are pushy or over-anxious, or who want to come and talk to you every day.)

◆ If there is an improvement in the pupil's work or behaviour after you have spoken to the parents, tell them so and thank them for their support, because they need to feel appreciated too.

◆ Keep a record of all contact with tutors, heads of year, and parents, including reward and sanction letters and phone calls.

Q6 Have a commitment to collaboration and cooperative working.

Suggestions for fulfilling Q6

◆ Always attend the year group planning meetings (primary) or subject planning meetings (secondary).

◆ If you teach science or ICT, make sure you follow the school's procedure for booking resources in plenty of time for the lab technician to organize them (secondary).

◆ For practical lessons, always finish your lesson five or ten minutes early to ensure that the classroom is left tidy and the chairs are up on the tables to make life easy for the cleaners. (Always stay on good terms with the cleaners; you might need to ask them to keep an eye open for small pieces of apparatus that get lost during the day.)

◆ Even if some support staff, such as classroom assistants (CAs), are not qualified, they are entitled to the same levels of politeness and kindness as the head and other teachers. If you set the example, the pupils should follow. If they don't, correct them instantly. It also increases the CAs' allegiance to you.

◆ If you have to work with a CA or a support teacher, possibly for children with SEN or EAL, make sure they have your plans in plenty of time and be prepared to spend some time with them to clarify which activities each of you will carry out. It is time well spent to create an easy working relationship.

◆ Chat to the special educational needs coordinator (SENCO) and ask him or her to explain the procedure for putting pupils on the special needs register and what support is given to them after that. If you strike up a positive working relationship, the SENCO may allow you to sit in on meetings with the educational welfare officer and educational psychologist.

◆ Keep your file of lesson plans up to date and make sure they provide details of how you work with other adults because they are evidence of your ability to work with others.

The following websites contain information helpful in connection with Q4, Q5 and Q6:

http://publications/everychildmatters.gov.uk

www.ttrb.ac.uk
www.tda.gov.uk/remodelling
www.ofsted.gov.uk/publications

Personal professional development

Q7(a) Reflect on and improve their practice, and take responsibility for identifying and meeting their developing professional needs.

Suggestions for fulfilling Q7(a)

◆ Until you become familiar with a class, show your lesson plans to your mentor or head of department (HOD) or class teacher and ask for suggestions to improve them.

◆ After each lesson, write an evaluation on the lesson plan, making at least one suggestion for improving it the next time you do it, and try to put it into practice as soon as you can.

◆ Likewise for feedback from lessons that have been observed. Try to use the feedback to improve your next lessons, and in your evaluation describe how your change of procedure has improved your lesson.

◆ After a difficult lesson, chat to other teachers as soon as possible and ask for suggestions on how to avoid similar difficulties in future.

◆ If you are not snowed under with marking, ask other teachers if you can sit in on their lessons during your non-contact periods, mentioning what particularly interests you. Experienced teachers do this.

◆ Even if it is not compulsory, ask if you can attend any staff INSET that takes place while you are on teaching practice.

◆ Carry out lesson observation activities suggested by your college and evaluate what you have learned from them. For example, observe a lesson just to see how the teacher manages difficult behaviour or manages to challenge the brightest.

◆ Spend some time looking at the Teacher Training Resource Bank (www.ttrb.ac.uk) for useful materials.

◆ Ask to look at the teachers' resources for your subjects in your school. You can never have too many ideas.

◆ Keep notes of new ideas and information. There is so much of it that you cannot possibly keep it all in your head.

Q7(b)   Identify priorities for their early professional development in the context of induction.

Suggestions for fulfilling Q7(b)

◆   Look at your own evaluations and the feedback you received on them from your mentor or class teacher. Do they match reasonably well? If so, it will reassure you that your judgement is realistic. You need to know what you are good at and what you need to work on to improve.

◆   Find what you are best at and look at the types of INSET that are available for that subject. It may be that when you finish your induction year, you can look for a post of responsibility or coordinator's post in that subject.

◆   Likewise, look at the areas where you are not so strong. INSET is for improving these areas as well.

◆   If you manage to find a job before your final teaching practice is over, you can start looking at the courses available in the local teachers' centre. Your prospective head will be pleased at your positive attitude to learning.

◆   Look at the website www.osiriseducational.co.uk. Osiris Educational runs really stimulating and interesting courses on how to improve the quality of your teaching. A day on one of its courses will send you away excited with new ideas of things to try out. Look also at courses run by BEAM and the Centre for Literacy in Primary Education, and some subject associations run courses for both primary and secondary teachers.

Q8   Have a creative and constructively critical approach towards innovation, being prepared to adapt their practice where benefits and improvements are identified.

Suggestions for fulfilling Q8

◆   Keep it clearly at the front of your mind that you never know it all. The longer you teach, the more you realize there is to learn. Show, by asking for advice and acting on it, that you are open to new ideas and willing to try new activities.

◆   Each time you try something new, sit down quietly on your own afterwards and think through the lesson. Make a note of everything that went well and that did not go well. Ask the class teacher or your mentor how you could improve.

◆   Remember that not all that is new is necessarily good. Don't forget that some traditional methods are worth retaining as well. Try to judge which practices work best. For each subject, keep a list of ideas and activities that went well and others that did not. It is important to develop the skill of sorting out the successful from the unsuccessful.

◆ Make judgements using the following criteria:
   − Did I achieve my objective with all or most of the class?
   − Did the pupils want to carry out the activities and learn?
   − Did they enjoy the lesson?
   − Did it spur them on to find anything else out on their own?
   If you give yourself a favourable answer to two or three of these questions, then your teaching was successful.

◆ Watch programmes on Teacher's TV. It is packed full of programmes that give practical advice in a user-friendly manner. All the programmes are available online.

Q9 Act upon advice and feedback and be open to coaching and mentoring.

Suggestions for fulfilling Q9

◆ Be ready to learn from everyone around you: teachers, lecturers, other students.

◆ When lecturers and teachers give you feedback on your lessons, ask them specifically to suggest activities and methods of teaching. Make a note of their advice, add it to your evaluation and try to put it into practice for a future lesson.

◆ Try to resist the temptation to feel that you are being put down by criticism, even if it is not very constructive. Try to follow advice from teachers. Even if it does not work, well, at least you have tried.

◆ Go to the planning meetings with other teachers in the year group and of course discuss plans with classroom assistants and anyone else who will be involved in delivering the lesson.

To help you with Q7(a), Q7(b), Q8 and Q9 you can download resources from the following websites to help you:

www.tda.gov.uk/teachers/induction/cedp.aspx
www.teachernet.gov.uk/professionaldevelopment/
   professionalassociations/teachingassociations
www.ttrb.ac.uk

www.citized.info
www.innovation-unit.co.uk
www.curee-paccts.com
www.teachers.tv

Professional knowledge

Look at this list when you are looking at topics for essays, assignments and projects. You may find a standard that coincides with a topic.

Teaching and learning

Q10   Have a knowledge and understanding of a range of teaching, learning and behaviour management strategies and know how to use and adapt them, including how to personalise learning and provide opportunities for all learners to achieve their potential.

Suggestions for fulfilling Q10

There is a wide range of strategies for teaching and learning. No list could possibly be complete but these make a start:

- ◆ To demonstrate your knowledge, show these on your lesson plan:
  - the objective
  - a mental and oral starter that recaps on a previous lesson and/or introduces the current lesson
  - a range of differentiated activities capable of challenging the brightest and providing support for the least able
  - a list of resources
  - the role of any support teacher or assistant working with you
  - a plenary that pulls the main teaching points of the lesson together.
- ◆ Start each lesson by writing the objective on the board and end by referring back to it and asking the pupils whether they think they have achieved it. Ask questions to check whether they have.
- ◆ During each lesson, include lots of questioning that draws the information from the pupils, rather than your spilling it all out to them. When pupils give an answer, try to draw out further information from them by asking for follow-up details.
- ◆ Distribute small whiteboards and dry-wipe pens. Ask the pupils to write down the answer and hold up their board. This ensures that

they all take part and makes it difficult for pupils to relax and let the others do the thinking.

◆ If you are asking questions that have a 50/50 answer, make them all answer by saying, 'Hands up for this option' and follow up with 'And hands up for this option.' It ensures that they all participate.

◆ Collaborative work can be an interesting way to introduce a new topic. Divide the class into mixed-ability groups and give them a task. For example, you could provide them with objects, books, pictures or information sheets and tell them what you want them to find out for themselves. Make it clear that they all have to feed back their findings to the class afterwards. Make sure each group has a bright, reliable pupil who will keep the rest on task.

◆ Use games where possible. Pupils, even the reluctant learners, love them.

◆ Interactive whiteboards are great for getting pupils interested; you can usually find a website to suit your lesson. However, be careful of using them all the time for every lesson. Don't forget the value of books, group-work, and learning through art and drama.

◆ Give homework that involves pupils finding things out for themselves by going to the library and looking up books and encyclopedias and using the internet. Emphasize to them that you want them to give their information in their own words. It is too easy for them to cut and paste information and present you with paragraphs that are of a standard of English which they could not have produced by themselves.

◆ Pair pupils who are not confident readers with a capable reader for the purposes of finding information.

◆ Give pupils opportunities to explain their ideas and methods to the class. For example, in maths lessons pupils love to explain their ways of working things out. Always emphasize the importance of treating other people's ideas and views with respect.

◆ Ask the class teacher whether any pupils have an individual educational programme (IEP) and study it. You will look efficient if you can include any of the details in your lesson.

Strategies for behaviour management

◆ Some teachers and students like to start with a class contract. They have a discussion about what teacher and pupils expect from each other and they write down the conclusions on a poster and everyone agrees to stick to them. This is only suitable on teaching practice if you have the class regularly, and once you have done it, you have to stick to your side of it, otherwise it falls apart at once. Always ask advice from your mentor or the regular teacher before you start, because it is important to know how the teachers in the school normally do it.

◆ Make clear from the start what you expect from the pupils by way of bringing the right books and equipment to class for each lesson.

◆ Try to start each lesson promptly. In a secondary school, meet and greet the pupils at the door so that they cannot dawdle up the corridor.

◆ Make eye contact with all pupils as they walk past you. Speak positively to any pupil who looks troubled or not his or her normal self.

◆ Establish a clear homework policy and stick to it.

◆ Don't shout (if you can possibly avoid it). Noisy teachers have noisy classes.

◆ In a primary school, to get attention from a noisy class, say, 'Hands up those you are listening.' Say, 'Well done' to the first six pupils who put their hands up. If it is an ultra-inattentive class, say, 'Well done, you can go out at break time' to the first six pupils.

◆ In a secondary school, you can establish a practice of saying, '3, 2, 1 and STOP.' Make it clear that you expect everyone's attention by the time you say '1', and anyone who is still moving or talking after you say 'STOP' will miss the first minute or two of the next break and carry it through.

◆ For the deliberately attention-seeking pupils, try to ignore the petty, negative behaviour (easier said than done, I know) and watch discreetly until they do the right thing. Then lavish praise on them.

For a few more suggestions to build up behaviour management strategies, see Q31. Also read *Getting the Buggers to Behave* by Sue Cowley (Continuum International). It is an entertaining and practical guide to building up a positive relationship with pupils and getting the best out of them.

The following websites contain information to help you:

www.standards.dfes.gov.uk/personalisedlearning
www.everychildmatters.gov.uk/ete/personalisedlearning
www.ofsted.gov.uk/publications
www.ttrb.ac.uk
www.citized.info

Assessment and monitoring

Q11   Know the assessment requirements and arrangements for the subjects/curriculum areas in the age ranges they are trained to teach, including those relating to public examinations and qualifications.

Suggestions for fulfilling Q11

◆ Ask to see the school's system for tracking their pupils' progress. Every school has its own arrangements, often stored on the computer system.
◆ Ask your mentor to explain his or her system for his or her subject.
◆ Study recent A level, GCSE, SATs and school or university entrance papers for your subject and age range. From these you should be able to make a list of skills necessary to pass the paper.
◆ Study the NC documents for your subjects and age range.
◆ If teachers are having assessment meetings, ask whether you can attend. If they have carried out assessments in your subject(s), ask whether you can look at some pupils' work along with the list of criteria for assessing. Try to assess a few papers by yourself, and then compare your assessment with the teachers'. Don't worry if you do not get it right straight away. Not many teachers do; it takes practice.

Q12   Know a range of approaches to assessment, including the importance of formative assessment.

Suggestions for fulfilling Q12

◆ Ask the teachers you work with to show you their methods of formative assessment and how it is recorded.
◆ At the end of each lesson, use the plenary session to ask questions to assess whether they have achieved the objective.
◆ If pupils have written the objective at the beginning of their independent work, ask them to show how well they think they have achieved it. In a primary school you can have a system of a smiling face for achieving it, sad face for not, and a face with a straight-line mouth if they are not sure. At secondary level they can tick, cross or write a question mark, or write a few words. You can then highlight it if you agree. It helps communication between you and your pupils if you know their perception of their progress.
◆ It is impossible to give each individual child oral feedback on all their work, but picking out the neediest for each piece and giving them some advice on how to improve often brings results.

◆ Try to find a time, as soon as you can after they have completed a piece of work, to give the class general feedback on that work. Remember, most forgetting takes place soon after the lesson.

◆ In each piece, pick out one issue for the child to work on to improve in their next piece of work.

◆ Explain the reason for the activities you are carrying out and, if it is not obvious, where they can use them in the real world.

◆ Keep at the front of your mind the fact that teachers are assessing pupils all the time and using their judgement to plan future lessons.

Q13   Know how to use local and national statistical information to evaluate the effectiveness of their teaching, to monitor the progress of those they teach and to raise levels of attainment.

Suggestions for fulfilling Q13

◆ Know where your school is. Look at the local league tables to see where your school lies. Then look at the national league table to see where the LEA lies. Of course, remember that if the school is in an affluent area and there are lots of professional parents, you should expect it to be higher up the table than one where there are lots of refugees, travellers, children on free school meals, children in care, and children who have entered the school unable to speak any English and who have not had full-time education since the age of 5. Remember that many schools in the lower half of the league table are doing a cracking good job coping with problems that do not exist in other schools.

◆ If they are available, look at past years' league tables to see whether the school is rising or falling, and try to work out why. It may be that the school is falling because it has had a sudden rise in its number of non-English-speaking refugees. It may be rising after the arrival of a new and innovative head.

◆ Look also at the value added tables. Try to work out the reason for the school's position in the league table. Has there been a high turnover of pupils? This can happen when the school is in the vicinity of a lot of accommodation for homeless people.

◆ Ask the teachers with whom you work to show you the statistical information about their learning: reading ages, spelling ages, stages of English for second language learners, verbal reasoning scores, stages on the special needs register, cognitive assessment scores, scores on maths assessments. They vary from school to school.

Study the figures to see whether patterns emerge. Ask teachers to explain how they use the information to set pupils' work.

◆ Chat to the SENCO and ask him or her to explain how he or she uses pupils' achievement to write their individual educational programme (IEP).

◆ Chat to the coordinator for English as an additional language and ask him or her to explain how he or she chose pupils to be focus pupils and set targets for them.

◆ Keep notes on what you learn as these may differ in detail between one school and another, and it is good to have a range of ideas.

◆ Look at how the school uses its own internal testing to set pupils' individual targets and write their IEPs.

◆ Keep at the front of your mind that this is a huge area and you cannot learn it all in a few weeks of a placement, so don't get stressed about it.

The following websites can provide information regarding Q11, Q12 and Q13:

www.aqa.org.uk
www.edexel.org.uk
www.ocr.org.uk
www.wiec.co.uk
www.ncsl.org.uk/useofdata

Subjects and curriculum

Q14 Have a secure knowledge and understanding of their subjects/ curriculum areas and related pedagogy to enable them to teach effectively across the age and ability range for which they are trained.

Suggestions for fulfilling Q14

◆ For secondary students on the PGCE or GTP programme, this point should be fulfilled by having a degree in your subject. Refer to any other relevant qualifications that you possess.

◆ For both primary and secondary B.Ed. students, you can point out that you are demonstrating your knowledge and understanding in an ongoing fashion throughout your teaching practice.

◆ Make sure that your objective is clear on your every lesson plan. Also, write in your evaluations how well you think you have achieved your objective. Give evidence for your judgement:

'Lower-ability pupils were able to explain . . .', 'Some higher-ability pupils were able to find out . . .'

◆ Primary teachers, who have to teach a wide range of subjects, may have to take small amounts of extra reading to prepare for individual subjects that were not the subject of their degree or A levels, because when teaching a subject you cannot cope by teaching at the limit of your own knowledge.

◆ When planning a sequence of lessons, try to build each one on the prior knowledge or skills learned in the previous one.

◆ Encourage pupils to ask questions when they do not understand something. When a pupil who is rather shy asks a question, start by saying, 'You are very sensible to ask . . .' or 'That's a good question.'

◆ When pupils have difficulty, try to break the point down into smaller points and go through them slowly to build up understanding.

◆ Never imagine that pupils know or understand something just because you have said it. Repetition and reinforcement are part of the process, even for able pupils.

◆ Have a set of questions prepared to test pupils' understanding.

◆ Ask questions to draw information from the pupils, rather than just spilling all the information and explanations out to them.

Q15 Know and understand the relevant statutory and non-statutory curricula and frameworks, including those provided through the National Strategies, for their subjects/curriculum areas, and other relevant initiatives applicable to the age and ability range for which they are trained.

Suggestions for fulfilling Q15

◆ Keep in good order all your lesson plans and evaluations, details of any of your assessments and records, and written feedback you have had from teachers or your college supervisor as these are evidence that you know your subject well and can teach it effectively.

◆ Read the National Curriculum documents for your subject(s) and/or age range.

◆ Read any documents that your college can suggest on the topics of inclusion, ICT and health and safety.

◆ Look at the topics for essays, assignments and projects. Are any of them related to your subject? Use your work on these to show that you know and understand the curriculum.

◆ Discuss the curriculum with your mentor and college supervisor to show your knowledge and understanding.

The following websites contain information that can help you:

www.nc.uk.net
www.ncaction.org.uk/index.htm
www.dfes.gov.uk
www.standards.dfes.gov.uk/local/clld

Literacy, numeracy and ICT

Q16 Have passed the professional skills tests in numeracy, literacy and information and communication technology (ICT).

Suggestions for fulfilling Q16

Get your registration number from your training provider and a list of centres where the tests may be taken.

Log on at www.tda.gov/skillstests to register and book a test. You may take each test as often as you wish, but you must pass them all before you can be awarded QTS, so it is wise to try the tests as soon as you can, before the pressure of exams and teaching practices starts building up. The tests are computerized and at the end you can see your results. If you have failed anything, you will be shown what you need to work on and how many more marks you need in order to pass. Print out the results and keep the record of your pass to show your training provider.

Q17 Know how to use skills in literacy, numeracy and ICT to support their teaching and wider professional activities.

Suggestions for fulfilling Q17

◆ Pupils will automatically be using reading and writing skills to learn other subjects. Try to ensure that pupils give you the same standard of literacy in their science, history, geography lessons as they would in English lessons.

◆ Keep it at the front of your mind that pupils also extend their literacy and numeracy skills in the process of learning other subjects. You can find opportunities to use maths across the curriculum: measuring in design and technology, scale in maps, capacity and timing in science experiments and timing in athletics.

◆ In subjects where the pupils learn a lot of new vocabulary, get them to make their own glossary at the back of their exercise books. Have them divide the last few pages of the book up into sections with a letter of the alphabet at the top of each section, so that when they meet a new word they can write it in the appropriate box, together with its meaning.

◆ Show on your lesson plans where you have asked the pupils to research topics on the internet.

◆ Give examples of your own resource and information sheets taken from the internet.

◆ You may be lucky and have access to a SMART Board for some lessons.

◆ Type up your worksheets and plans on the computer. Most schools have got a skeleton plan for you to type onto. This sometimes saves you time because if certain things are the same each week, the next week's plan can be superimposed on it.

◆ Type labels for displays and add small pieces of clip art.

◆ If you prepare work at home, you can email it from your home email address to the school. Some schools do not allow you to put plans on disk and bring them into the school in case you bring a virus into the school computer system.

◆ When you go on a school trip or school journey, take the school's digital camera and take lots of photos to download onto the computer and use as a stimulus for discussion, for pupils to use to illustrate their work, to use on a PowerPoint display in the class assembly or simply to give to the pupils as souvenirs. It's great for keeping up the enthusiasm.

◆ Use PowerPoint to illustrate lessons or assemblies.

◆ Use spreadsheets with pupils' names and a list of skills or tasks to record what they have completed.

◆ When able pupils have poor handwriting, allow them to type their work onto the computer. It saves them frustration and makes it a lot easier for you to read.

The following websites contain information to help you:

www.tda.gov.uk/skillstests
http://schools.org.uk
www.teachers.tv
www.ngfl.gov.uk
www.ttrb.ac.uk

Achievement and diversity

Q18   Understand how children and young people develop and that the progress and well-being of learners are affected by a range of developmental, social, religious, ethnic, cultural and linguistic influences.

Suggestions for fulfilling Q18

◆   Look at your choice of essay titles. Is there one on the effect of these background influences on a child's learning? A well-thought-out essay should demonstrate that you understand the effects of home background on learning.

◆   Do you have to carry out an assignment or project involving small-scale research? You could design one as part of your coursework and so kill two birds with one stone. If you are in a multicultural school, look at your class list and that of another student. Make a table as in Table 1 of the classes setting out:
    ◆   their National Curriculum levels for English
    ◆   their mother tongue
    ◆   the number of years they have been learning English
    ◆   whether they are on free school meals – a clear sign of poverty
    ◆   whether they are on the SEN register
    ◆   whether their parents are competent speakers of English
    ◆   whether the parents were educated in the UK

The more classes and the greater range of classes with which you do this, the more reliable your results will be, but for the purpose of the course you will probably have time to look at only two or three classes.

You can then study the results and look for patterns from which you can draw conclusions. In analysing the results, answer one or two of the following questions and suggest reasons for your conclusions.

1.   Is a pupil's intellectual ability the main or only reason for success or failure within the system?
2.   How does poverty (free school lunches) affect a child's progress?
3.   Do EAL children learn more quickly if their parents speak English or were educated in the UK?
4.   Do the pupils who have come into school speaking very little English catch up with or overtake the children who were born in the UK? Why? Why not?
5.   Does having lots of friends or no friends make a difference to the child's attitude to work and success as a learner?

Table 1 Grid showing conditions that can influence a pupil's learning

Pupils' names	NC level of English	Stage of English 1/2/3/4/	Mother tongue	No. of years learning Eng.	SEN register (Y/N)	Parents fully competent in English (Y/N)	Parents educated in UK (Y/N)	Has at least two friends in class (Y/N)

6.   What other factors play a part in influencing a pupil's learning?

When finishing your analysis, remember to add a paragraph stating that your findings are indicators of reasons for achievement or lack of it. Add that you must bear in mind that to be absolutely conclusive in your statements you would need a survey of a few thousand pupils, which is not within the scope of a small-scale piece of research.

Note: You should only attempt the above if it also fulfils the requirement for an essay or other piece of academic work. You cannot possibly afford the time for it otherwise.

Q19   Know how to make effective personalised provision for those they teach, including those for whom English is an additional language or who have special educational needs or disabilities, and how to take practical account of diversity and promote equality and inclusion in their teaching.

Suggestions for fulfilling Q19

◆   For each class, ask the teacher to give you a class list with all of the data concerning SEN, EAL and their stages of English, and enquire how he or she differentiates the work for them.
◆   If you are fortunate to have a support teacher for EAL or SEN to help you, ask his or her advice as well.
◆   If you have pupils who are gifted and talented, add to the lesson plan a task to extend them – something to find out for themselves when they have finished the task set.
◆   Put a Shap multicultural calendar of religious festivals on a class noticeboard and point out the festivals as they come round.
◆   Include a religious festival in your RE lessons (if applicable).
◆   Put up a multicultural display at an appropriate time.
◆   Use an assembly to inform about a current festival of another religion.
◆   Ask pupils to explain to the class how they have celebrated a recent festival such as Eid, or Chinese or Jewish New Year.
◆   Try to pronounce their names correctly and avoid the temptation to give them a simplified (shortened or Anglicized) version of their name. I have known teachers to cause offence unwittingly by doing so.
◆   If a parents' night comes round, ask if you can take part or at least sit in on the interview. If it is a long placement or you are in a school for most of a year, doing the GTP course, try to build up a

positive relationship with as many parents as you can. They can be a great source of support for the teacher.

◆ Be a good listener. Pupils love it. If you are on playground or corridor duty, pupils often love to come and talk to you. It is an opportunity to build up a relationship with pupils, and time well spent.

Q20   Know and understand the roles of colleagues with specific responsibilities, including those with responsibility for learners with special educational needs and disabilities and other individual learning needs.

Suggestions for fulfilling Q20

◆ Ask your mentor to introduce you to the SENCO and EAL coordinator and ask for the IEPs of the pupils whom you teach.
◆ Read the school's anti-bullying policy and, obviously, stick to it as closely as you can.
◆ Strike up a friendly working relationship with any teaching assistants or support teachers who support pupils in class.
◆ Ask their advice on coping with pupils. In some schools the teaching assistants have been there longer than the teachers; they have built up a long-standing relationship of trust and are very competent at dealing with pupils.

The following websites contain information to help you:

www.nc.uk.net
www.citized.info
www.standards.dfes.gov.uk/ethnicminorities
www.standards.dfes.gov.uk/genderachievement

Health and well-being

Q21(a) Be aware of current legal requirements, national policies and guidance on the safeguarding and promotion of the well-being of children and young people.

Suggestions for fulfilling Q21(a)

◆ Read the *Every Child Matters* criteria.
◆ Read the school's policy on pastoral care. It should explain the school's chain of command for dealing with issues such as discipline and bullying.

◆ Ask who is the designated teacher for reporting to concerning children at risk. It is often, but not always, the headteacher.

◆ Report to him or her anything that makes you suspect that a child is being abused.

◆ You must respect the confidentiality of anything you are told about pupils, and the Child Protection Register. In some schools, teachers are not told unless they teach the pupil.

Q21(b) Know how to identify and support children and young people whose progress, development or well-being is affected by changes or difficulties in their personal circumstances, and when to refer them to colleagues for specialist support.

Suggestions for fulfilling Q21(b)

◆ Ask the class teacher whether there is anything you should know about pupils' home life or special circumstances. Ask whether there is any pupil who lives in care or has suffered family breakdown or bereavement.

◆ Ask what the school's policy for coping with the pupil's difficulty is.

◆ When a child is in great distress, for example from bereavement, and unable to concentrate on learning, it is counter-productive to insist that they work. Not only will you fail to make them work but you will destroy your relationship with them for the future. In such cases, I always say, 'If you cannot cope just now, that's fine, I understand. You can get a book and read.' This has the dual advantage that the pupil is actually doing something educational – reading lifts the pupil's mind above his or her troubles – and you have built a positive relationship with the pupil for the future.

The following websites contain information to help you:

www.everychildmatters.gov.uk
www.teachernet.gov.uk/wholeschool/behaviour/tacklingbullying

Professional skills

Planning

Q22 Plan for progression across the age and ability range for which they are trained, designing effective learning sequences within lessons and across series of lessons and demonstrating secure subject/curriculum knowledge.

Suggestions for fulfilling Q22

◆ You should be able to prove you can do the planning referred to in Q22 by presenting a detailed file of lessons for the placement. Each lesson should have an objective that includes the National Curriculum reference. It should state the pupils' prior experience and what they will move on to next. Activities planned should be described in detail and differentiated, and you should have a method of assessing how well the pupils have achieved the objective, for example by the use of questioning. Your evaluations show that you have reflected on how the lesson went and how it could be improved.

◆ Attend the year group or subject planning meetings.

Q23 Design opportunities for learners to develop their literacy, numeracy and ICT skills.

Suggestions for fulfilling Q23

◆ Look closely at your lesson plans for literacy and numeracy. Make sure each states the National Curriculum objective and that it shows clearly how the work is differentiated and how you assess whether you have achieved the objective. Put in an extra, challenging activity for the higher-ability pupils. In your evaluation, suggest ways of improving the lesson.

ICT skills are also built up by integrating them with lessons across the curriculum. The following are a few suggestions that can be adapted for different topics and age groups:

◆ For history and geography, you can find an interesting website about a topic that the pupils are studying and make up a list of information for them to retrieve from it.

◆ For science investigations, for example measuring the length of a shadow at different times of the day, let pupils construct a table on the computer so that they can put in their findings and use them to construct a graph, either on the computer or by hand.

◆ For English, ask pupils to type the first draft of their essays or poems, which you can then annotate with suggestions for improvement. I have found pupils very willing to edit their work to improve it without the painful task of rewriting it. When the task is complete, let them look on the internet, at clip art or at the school's files if appropriate to find illustrations.

◆ For poetry writing lessons, try www.gigglepoetry.com, an effective site for getting Key Stage 2 reluctant poets started. They have interesting fun activities for making up poems and competitions.

◆ For maths, there are games on the internet that you can use. Try http://puzzlemaker.discoveryeducation.com for a selection of games and puzzles.

◆ There are also websites that prepare worksheets for lots of topics, PowerPoint displays and interactive games on National Curriculum topics. I have found the following particularly useful:

www.primaryresources.co.uk
www.bbc.co.uk/schools/revisewise
www.bbc.co.uk/skillswise
www.topmarks.co.uk
www.mathszone.co.uk
www.ngfl-cymru.org.uk

If you use a website on the IWB, write the details on the board for the pupils to copy into their diaries, or copy and paste it for them to try out at home if they have access to a computer.

Q24   Plan homework or other out-of-class work to sustain learners' progress and to extend and consolidate their learning.

Suggestions for fulfilling Q24

◆ Read the school's homework policy and try to stick to it.
◆ Always write details of the homework on your plan.
◆ Differentiate the tasks.
◆ Give homework tasks that involve pupils consulting books from the library and the internet to find information for themselves.
◆ Ask your mentor whether most pupils have their own computer at home, and, if they have, give them the option to type their homework. The school may have provision for pupils to use school computers at lunch time. Typing has the advantage that when you mark it, or annotate it to suggest improvements, the pupils can edit their work. Pupils like this because they can improve their work easily, without spoiling the appearance of it.

◆ Try to give them tasks that are easier to do at home than in school. For example, in maths ask them to choose a few containers in the kitchen and guess their capacity and the measure, and write their estimate and measurements. They can do the same with weighing and measuring lengths. In geography lessons, pupils can look up weather temperatures in newspapers for studies on climate. Key Stage 1 pupils learning about shape can look for things in the home or environment that are round, square, rectangular and so on.

◆ Suggest a time limit on their work, for example half an hour, and tell them to write the time taken at the end of the work.

◆ On parents' evenings, ask the parents to check that their children have done their homework and encourage them with praise for work well done.

◆ When pupils regularly do not bring their homework to school, ask the teacher whether the parents are likely to support you in ensuring that they do it, before asking the parents to check up on their child. Some schools ask parents to sign the pupils' homework to show that they have supervised it.

The following websites contain information to help you:

www.standards.dfes.gov.uk
www.parentscentre.gov.uk
www.becta.org.uk
www.bbc.co.uk/schools

Teaching

The next number is densely detailed and requires a lot of practice to get right, so do not fall into the trap of thinking that you are failing if everything does not fall into place quickly. You could not possibly do all of the following in any one lesson.

For Q25(a–d) it is important to keep all of your lesson plans, evaluations and samples or photocopies of pupils' work and photographs so you can use them as evidence.

Sometimes pupils enjoy a lesson so much that they go off and find out extra things for themselves, or do some extra work on a topic. If this happens, then you can feel very proud of yourself as this is a clear sign you are doing well. Praise the pupil lavishly and make sure you keep a photocopy or record of any extra work pupils do, as it is evidence that you can inspire your pupils.

Q25   Teach lessons and sequences of lessons across the age and ability range for which they are trained in which they:

(a)   use a range of teaching strategies and resources, including e-learning, taking practical account of diversity and promoting equality and inclusion.

Suggestions for fulfilling Q25(a)
Before you start teaching lessons:

◆   First ask the teacher for lots of information about what the pupils have already done and ask for suggestions regarding the next step.
◆   Look through a range of the pupils' exercise books to get an overall picture of the standard.
◆   Show the teacher your lesson plan and ask whether there is anything you have left out and for suggestions for improvement.
◆   Ask which pupils need extra support and which need an extra-challenging activity to stretch them.

Planning and teaching lessons
For a collection of ideas for interesting lessons, let me recommend the *100 Ideas* set of books published by Continuum International. There is a handy paperback book for each subject, packed with practical suggestions.

◆   Start simple. When you are feeling comfortable with one type of lesson, then try another and build up your range of teaching strategies gradually.
◆   If using a group activity, remember that ability grouping is not the only way to organize the groups. Collaborative activities should have a bright and fairly sensible child in each group. EAL children should not all be in the same group because they absorb a lot of English from indigenous pupils around them. It is ideal to have beginners in English in the same group as pupils who speak their native language as well as English.
◆   Mark clearly on the lesson plan any extra provision for SEN, EAL, gifted and talented children.
◆   Make a list of resources for the lesson and have them marked on your lesson plan.
◆   Talk to any support staff in advance to make sure the details are clear to them.

◆ Pupils remember best what they find out or deduce for themselves. If you are introducing a new topic in history or geography, put them into groups to study a set of pictures, write down all the information they have deduced, and, in their groups, report it back to the class.

◆ They also remember better the start and finish of each lesson, so make sure you have an interesting starter and plenary. Try to make the plenary fun so that the pupils leave the lesson on an 'up'.

◆ Children and teenagers are great performers. Giving them the opportunity to address the class builds up their confidence and self-esteem.

◆ If a lesson goes well, you can extend it by setting a 'research' task to carry out at home. This may be optional if the pupils already have their full complement of homework. Always reward with praise, stars, house points etc. all the pupils who complete a voluntary task.

◆ Remember that much good learning takes place outside the school. Always reward ostentatiously any extra work that children do without being prompted by parents or teachers.

(b) build on prior knowledge, develop concepts and processes, enable learners to apply new knowledge, understanding and skills and meet learning objectives.

Suggestions for fulfilling Q25(b)

◆ Make sure the objective is clear at the start of each lesson. Write it on the board and explain it.

◆ On your plan, write the section and number of the objective that you are fulfilling.

◆ Start lessons with a warm-up that recaps information from the previous lesson or revises necessary skills or concepts for the lesson in hand.

◆ Encourage pupils by showing or describing occasions when one could use the new knowledge or skills in the real world.

◆ Where possible, try to introduce an element of ICT into your lessons. For example, let them type their work, especially if they have poor handwriting; or find additional information from the internet; or illustrate it with pictures, maps or diagrams from clip art.

◆ If you have an IWB, you can often find a website with illustrated information or an interactive activity or game that makes the lesson more interesting. Most schools have a shared folder where you can put work for the children during their ICT lesson.

◆ If any pupils have an IEP, see whether you can include one of their points in the lesson. It will not be possible to do this in every lesson, but it will impress the teacher if you can include it occasionally.

◆ In your evaluation, make a note of anything that pupils find difficult and put it in the warm-up for a future lesson.

◆ Look at the school's target-setting procedure to check that you are using it correctly. Ask your teacher-mentor for help.

(c) adapt their language to suit the learners they teach, introducing new ideas and concepts clearly, and using explanations, questions, discussions and plenaries effectively.

Suggestions for fulfilling Q25(c)

◆ If there are second language learners in the class, start each lesson by picking out the key vocabulary and making sure the pupils understand it. Always write new vocabulary on the board, with its meaning.

◆ Don't just explain the facts and concepts; try to draw the information out of them by asking questions.

◆ As the lesson progresses, ask questions to check that the pupils understand, because sometimes they are shy of asking in front of a whole class. And, of course, always praise pupils for their sensible, mature attitude when they ask you to explain something they did not understand.

◆ Be a good listener when pupils give explanations and encourage the pupils to listen to each other.

◆ Never allow pupils to laugh at or ridicule other pupils, no matter how far wrong they may be.

◆ Try to correct wrong answers constructively. 'That's half right' or 'That's a reasonable guess' is much less discouraging than 'No, that's wrong.' When an answer is completely wrong, say 'No' gently. Pupils who are unsure of themselves are easily put down.

◆ In your plenary, include an activity or line of questions that show you whether the pupil has grasped the point of the lesson.

◆ Simple language of explanation works best.

(d) demonstrate the ability to manage the learning of individuals, groups and whole classes, modifying their teaching to suit the stage of the lesson.

Suggestions for fulfilling Q25(d)

◆ If a lesson contains several activities, time management is important. Write the timings for every activity on the lesson plan. Remember that the lesson plan is a servant, not a master. You may find that something takes longer than you had anticipated and some of the lesson needs to be put off until the next lesson. Remember, it is the quality that matters. It is better to do three-quarters of a lesson well and write in the evaluation that the remainder will be completed in the next lesson than complete all of it inadequately.

◆ Remember that pupils with SEN or EAL may understand more than they can put down on paper. If you prepare a simplified cloze procedure sheet, which they can fill in, it prevents them from suffering the frustration of having to do too much writing.

◆ Give these pupils plenty of opportunities to give oral explanations.

◆ Often they can type better than they can write, so if you let them do their independent work on the computer, it is satisfying for both pupils and teacher.

◆ Make sure the list of resources is on the lesson plan and check them off as you set the lesson up. Where possible, it is best to have the equipment on the tables before the pupils come into the classroom.

◆ At the end of the lesson, always insist that pupils collect resources and pack everything away tidily.

◆ If you have other adults supporting in the lesson, have their role clearly marked on the plan, discuss it with them beforehand and thank them afterwards.

◆ To extend the more able, set them a short but interesting task involving finding out something for themselves.

◆ Always praise pupils warmly and reward them with house points, stars or stickers for any work that they have done by themselves without being asked.

◆ When asking questions, have pupils explain their view to their partners before you ask someone to explain their answer to the class.

◆ Look at your lesson plan to see whether there is anything that is culture based, such as religious festivals, and explain their importance early on in the lesson.

◆ If pupils draw you off the subject and the lesson goes off at a tangent, keep an eye on the objective. It will not matter if the lesson does not go exactly as you had planned it, as long as the objective is achieved.

◆ In the plenary, refer back to the objective to check that all or most of the pupils have achieved it.

The following websites can help you:

www.standards.dfes.gov.uk
www.standards.dfes.gov.uk/ethnicminorities
www.standards.dfes.gov.uk/genderandachievement
www.standards.dfes.gov.uk/personalisedlearning
www.teachernet.gov.uk
www.ncaction.org.uk/index.htm
www.nc.uk.net
www.becta.org.uk
www.ttrb.ac.uk
www.teachernet.gov.uk/publications

Assessing, monitoring and giving feedback

Q26(a) Make effective use of a range of assessment, monitoring and recording strategies.

Suggestions for fulfilling Q26(a)

◆ Ask your mentor to explain the school's procedure for assessment, monitoring and recording, and, of course, try to use it.

◆ Before each lesson, write down a few questions that you will ask during the plenary to test whether pupils have achieved the objective.

◆ During the lesson, explain to the pupils how the task in hand helps them to achieve the objective, if it is not obvious.

◆ If the pupils are taking a National Curriculum test, such as SATs or QCA optional tests, and the teachers mark them in-house, ask to be involved in the marking, or at least read the teachers' manual. Try to assess pupils' work against the National Curriculum level descriptors. Compare your assessments against those of the teachers. This is a task that you can learn to do only by practice.

◆ Ask several teachers to explain their assessment strategies, because you need a range of ideas.

Q26(b) Assess the learning needs of those they teach in order to set challenging learning objectives.

Suggestions for fulfilling Q26(b)

◆ Ask the teacher to help you at first because it is impossible to get this one right without knowing the class. In practice, it is likely that the teacher will decide the objectives for you.

◆ Read the school's policy for target setting and try to fit in with it.

◆ On your plans, along with the objective write in the National Curriculum section its number.

◆ At the end of the lesson or unit, ask the pupils to refer back to the objective and decide whether they have achieved it. Write beside it a smiling face if they believe they have achieved it, a sad face if not, and a face with a straight mouth if they are unsure. When you mark the books, highlight this symbol if you agree with them and write a comment if you don't. For you, this is an effective way of keeping tabs on the pupils' learning, and it is reassuring for the pupils to know that they have judged correctly.

◆ In your evaluation, comment on how many pupils you believe have achieved the objective, and what you must do for the others in the next lesson.

◆ With older pupils it may in some cases be appropriate to ask them to suggest what they might try next.

Q27 Provide timely, accurate and constructive feedback on learners' attainment, progress and areas for development.

Suggestions for fulfilling Q27

◆ Read the school's policy for marking pupils' work before you start, and stick to it as closely as you can. Pupils like consistency.

◆ Always mark books before they are handed back, otherwise you will give the impression that the work is not important.

◆ Try to make your marking advisory as well as congratulatory. Write one or two positive comments and then pick out the most obvious error and write it as a target for a future piece.

◆ Rather than mark every single error with glaring red ink, pick out one or two points for the pupil to work on.

Q28 Support and guide learners to reflect on their learning, identify the progress they have made and identify their emerging learning needs.

Suggestions for fulfilling Q28

◆ When giving oral feedback to the class, do it as soon as you can after they have completed the work. Remember that most forgetting takes place soon after the work is done.

◆ If pupils are shy or self-conscious in front of others, try to speak to them quietly on their own. A few words of encouragement can work wonders.

◆ If a pupil is losing confidence, show him or her the work at the front of the book and the work at the end to show progress. Reassure the pupil that he or she has improved and can make the same improvement again.

◆ About once a term, instead of hearing pupils reading, go through their last piece of writing with them individually to point out errors and give them advice as to how to improve in the next piece. They will love the attention.

◆ Never make criticism wholly negative. Give the positive bit first and if a pupil looks dejected, finish on a positive note. Keeping a pupil interested is of paramount importance.

◆ At the end of term, ask the pupils to write a list of the things they have improved during the term, and a list of the things they think they should work on in the following term. Write a positive, encouraging note on each pupil's book.

The following websites contain information to help you:

www.ioea.org.uk
www.ncsl.org.uk/useofdata
www.learntolearn.ac.uk
www.innovation-unit.co.uk

Reviewing teaching and learning

Q29   Evaluate the impact of their teaching on the progress of all learners, and modify their planning and classroom practice where necessary.

Suggestions for fulfilling Q29

◆ No one could get this all right first time. After each lesson, mentally reflect on it and decide what went well, what needs to be revised and what could be added to improve it. Write it in your evaluation and try to act on it next time.

◆ Ask the teacher who normally teaches the class to give you his or her frank opinion of how well the pupils are performing for you. Emphasize that you are eager to get things right. Compare the teacher's judgement with your own.

◆ Look at the results of any end-of-unit assessments you have done with the class. Compare them with any that have been done previously by the teacher.

◆ Look carefully at results that do not look as good as you had hoped and find opportunities to revise the work in future lessons. Keep your results as evidence that you can see the link between your pupils' progress and the quality of your teaching, and act on that evidence.

◆ After a few weeks of your placement, look back over work in the pupils' books and see whether there is progress. Note especially whether there is any evidence that the pupils have acted on any advice you have given in your feedback or marking.

The following websites contain information to help you:

www.qca.org.uk
www.tre.ngfl.gov.uk
www.teachers.tv

Learning environment
Q30   Establish a purposeful and safe learning environment conducive to learning and identify opportunities for learners to learn in out-of-school contexts.

Suggestions for fulfilling Q30
◆ Read the school's safety policy and, obviously, make sure you stick to the last letter of it. If you are uncertain about the details, ask a teacher.

◆ If you are about to take a lesson that could have an element of danger, say in science or technology, make sure you have asked the regular teacher for details about any procedures about the handling of hacksaws, glue guns, Stanley knives, acids and telescopes if out of doors.

◆ You should not, while a student, have to organize a school trip, but you may well have to go on one. If one is due to be undertaken, it is worthwhile to offer to go on it to learn the ropes. Teachers will be pleased that you are willing. Read the school policy before you go. Take a digital camera and take lots of photos to use for follow-up work.

◆ You probably will not have to fill in a risk assessment form, but still ask to see one so you can see how it is done, because you might have to do one during your induction year.

◆ Discuss the events of the trip with pupils, using the digital photos as reminders. Compare the quality of the pupils' follow-up work with their normal standard. I often find an improvement after a day trip, and if there is one, this should show the value of the trip. Keep examples or photocopies of pupils' work as evidence.

◆ Often after trips, pupils are stimulated to go and find out things for themselves. If this happens, make a note of details and use them as evidence of your effectiveness.

◆ As soon as you come back, make a list of everything you have learned about procedures, while it is still fresh in your mind.

◆ Try to find opportunities to use the school's outdoor environment. It may be a suitable place for still life sketching, pond-dipping, Sun and shadows, apparent Sun movements, or maths games to learn north, south, east and west.

◆ You cannot overstate safety instructions with pupils. Don't be afraid to repeat them.

Q31   Establish a clear framework for classroom discipline to manage learners' behaviour constructively and promote their self-control and independence.

Suggestions for fulfilling Q31

Class discipline or behaviour management is a huge topic. Teachers have written whole books on it. The points below will help you lay down the foundations for effective class management and help you avoid some of the pitfalls.

◆ Early on in your placement, ask to read the school's behaviour policy, because it is easier to control pupils if you are following the same set of rules as everyone else.

◆ Ask the teacher or teachers who normally teach the class(es) to explain their behaviour management strategies. Consistency is the keyword. Of course, if you are in a secondary school, you may find they differ in detail. Remember that classes, individual pupils and teachers differ, so you need a range of strategies; no one size fits all.

◆ Read the section on behaviour management again to remind yourself of details you have forgotten.

◆ Always be prepared to the last letter. It avoids giving pupils the opportunity to misbehave.

◆ For potentially difficult classes, if you intend using a lot of equipment it is doubly important that you have it set out on tables before the pupils come in. Doing so not only saves lesson time but also lessens their chances of distracting others while you get organized.

◆ It is never enough simply to deliver lessons; you have to build up a respectful relationship with the pupils. Listen to them; show them that you consider them and their education to be important. Speak quietly but firmly, and above all never use sarcasm.

◆ When one pupil is trying to distract another, praise lavishly the pupils who are ignoring the distracter. Tell them you are impressed by their grown-up attitude and ability to ignore babyish behaviour. Reward them with house points, stars or stickers and tell them you will give them more every time they ignore the stupid behaviour. It often quashes the distracter.

◆ Make lessons as interesting as you can, with an element of fun.

◆ Prepare more than you think you will need. If you run out of activities, the devil will soon find work for bored pupils.

◆ Never let one pupil spoil it for the whole class. For the disruptive pupil who is determined to wreck the class and ignores your warnings, you might say, 'You are clearly not in control of yourself and you are spoiling other pupils' opportunity to learn. Stand on the other side of the classroom door/sit on the carpet until you have calmed down and are capable of behaving like a mature Year 6 [or whatever] pupil. When you have done that you can return and we will say no more about it.'

◆ For classes that take a long time to tidy up at the end of a practical lesson, establish a practice of letting the first group that is ready go out for break time a minute or two before the others.

◆ If necessary, reorganize seating so that pupils can be moved away from others who distract them from their work.

◆ Make sure all pupils are placed so that they can comfortably see the board.

◆ For the deliberately attention-seeking pupils, try to ignore the petty, negative behaviour (easier said than done, I know) and watch discreetly until they do the right thing. Then lavish praise on them.

◆ For the class that is reluctant to work, establish an incentive scheme, such as dividing them into four groups and letting them suggest a snazzy name for their own group. Then put up a chart with their group names and give points for good behaviour or effort or punctuality and a reward at the end of the week or month for the group with the most points.

◆ For pupils who like to ignore the teacher, I have a system: ask politely, tell firmly, and then deliver a threat such as a missed break-time – and carry it out if necessary. It works most of the time after you have carried out the threat a time or two. If you keep pupils in for a whole break-time, always let them out five minutes before the end to go to the loo and have a drink and some fresh air. With many pupils, giving them no break at all can make them worse instead of better.

◆ Keep the classroom tidy. Give pupils responsibilities for looking after different areas or types of equipment. Remember, a disorderly environment sends out the message that the work is not important.

◆ Keep the display boards attractive, displaying the children's work neatly mounted with their name clearly displayed. This sends out the message that their work is valued and fosters a pride in their achievement (most of the time).

The following websites contain information to help you:

www.behaviour4learning.ac.uk
www.dfes.gov.uk/wholeschoolbehaviour/tacklingbullying
www.teachernet.gov.uk/teachingandlearning/resourcematerials/
outsideclassroom

Team working and collaboration
Q32 Work as a team member and identify opportunities for working with colleagues, sharing the development of effective practice with them.

Suggestions for fulfilling Q32
◆ Keep it clear in your mind that teamwork is a vital element of success in any school, so it is important to strike up a positive working relationship with all school staff – cleaners, school maintenance staff like the school keeper, kitchen staff and mid-day supervisors, secretary, school nurse. Never fall into the trap of thinking that they are less important than the teaching staff and need less consideration. Treat them with the same respect and politeness as you give the head and you will be surprised at the many small ways in which they make your job run more smoothly.

◆ When you start, ask the teachers to check your lesson plans and offer suggestions.

◆ Ask them to give you feedback on any lessons they observe.

Emphasize that you are eager to learn and appreciate having your mistakes pointed out to you.

◆ It is good practice to include the support staff in your planning where appropriate, and take time in advance to explain activities in detail to the teaching assistants (TAs). Always thank them afterwards as they will support you more enthusiastically if they know they are valued.

◆ Always ensure that the role of the TA, SEN or EAL teacher is clearly marked on the lesson plan.

Q33   Ensure that colleagues working with them are appropriately involved in supporting learning and understand the roles they are expected to fulfil.

Suggestions for fulfilling Q33

◆ Discuss pupils' progress with the support teacher.

◆ After several lessons, take time to look at pupils' work with and without the support teacher. Compare the two. The comparison should give you a fair idea about the value of the support teacher's work.

◆ Ask the support teacher's guidance in recording and monitoring pupils' progress. Let the support teacher see that you value his or her judgement.

◆ Ask to be allowed to sit in on planning meetings, if not already invited.

◆ As always, discuss lesson plans with the support teacher before the lesson.

◆ Always take time to establish a friendly, working relationship with all SEN, EAL and any other support teachers and classroom assistants over coffee in the staffroom.

◆ Ask the teacher whether you can sit in on interviews with the educational psychologist (EP) and educational welfare officer (EWO) to learn about their roles.

The following websites contain information to help you:

http://publications.everychildmatters.gov.uk
www.teachers.tv
www.ttrb.ac.uk

And when you have waded your way through this little lot, reward yourself with a smashing night out!

4 | The side issues

What is stress?

According to my dictionary, stress is mental and physical distress or anxiety caused by difficult circumstances. It is not something imagined by students and others. It is real and some students suffer it very badly.

Today's students probably suffer from it more than students in previous generations, because of the added pressures of finding cash to pay their fees and keep, and the thought of their loans hanging over them like a sword of Damocles long after they qualify. On the other hand, there are more systems in place now for students to get help before they reach crisis point.

What causes students to become stressed?

The following are a few of the difficult circumstances that can cause you, as a student, to suffer anxiety:

◆ Being unable to finish assignments or dissertations on time.
◆ Fearing you cannot understand the work or present essays of high enough quality.
◆ Dreading not being able to manage the pupils the next day on your school placement.
◆ Coping with the workload on teaching practice. As soon as you shift one pile of marking, another appears.
◆ Lack of support in schools.
◆ Fearing the reaction of your family if you fail.
◆ Living in unpleasant accommodation.
◆ Money problems.
◆ Having family problems: unruly children, illness in the family, bereavement.
◆ Discovering that there is a shortage of jobs for your area of study.

(Fortunately, at the moment this is not usually a problem for student teachers.)

Stress is usually caused by a mixture of some of the above.

How do you recognize the signs?

A small amount of stress in our lives keeps us all moving, working and achieving, but there is a limit to how much of it we can tolerate, and when we have substantially more than we can cope with, it makes us ill.

Unlike a dose of a normal disease, stress creeps up on you so slowly that you don't know it is happening until it is too late. It is important to recognize the signs in time and try to avoid the resulting unhappiness. It is also worth being aware of the frame of mind of people around you so that if one of your friends or colleagues is suffering it, you may be able to step in and help them.

Stress takes different forms, but these are common symptoms:

◆ frequent headaches
◆ extreme tiredness
◆ a feeling of powerlessness
◆ fear that your life is out of control
◆ experiencing panic attacks at times
◆ wanting to cry or actually sitting down and doing so at inappropriate times
◆ feeling depressed – morbidly unhappy with a mood of inadequacy
◆ feeling that life is not worth living

How do you avoid stress?

Being organized is crucial in the avoidance of stress. A lot of stress is caused by poor time management and weak organizational skills.

When you are given a new essay or assignment, it is important to consult the calendar before the textbooks. Look up the date for handing it in and plan ahead. Aim to finish with at least a week to spare, because these things often take longer than you expect.

You should also build into your timetable a few days to reread, check and amend the essay. Also remember that if lots of students are reliant on textbooks in the library, it is unwise to leave your essay until the last week because the books will be in demand.

If you have written an essay or completed an assignment but are not feeling confident about it, you could ask the lecturer to look at it before you formally hand it in. Some lecturers are willing to read students' work if they have it in time and tell them where they have gone wrong or could make a few improvements — or even just give the reassurance that the essay is fine. Of course it is important to give the lecturer the work well in advance of the deadline date, and it is well worth doing so for the peace of mind it brings.

During teaching practice, self-organization becomes doubly important because if you don't sort out your lessons and resources, you will lose control and credibility and become stressed and grease the slippery slope to failure. Before you leave each day, it is a sensible precaution to make sure you are prepared for the following day's lessons. Never live hand-to-mouth because you will always find things that you cannot do at the last minute and you will wish you had sorted them out sooner.

Routine

Plan out your week. Having times designated for socializing and times for working is much better than just taking each day as it comes or waiting until you are in the mood for working. On teaching practice, build a marking and planning space into the daily routine.

When facing up to the fact that you might not have much spare time for yourself during the week, make sure you set aside time at the weekends and holidays. It is important to learn to shut school or college out of your mind for a period every weekend to enable you to return to the job refreshed.

Half-term

If you have one, set aside a bit of time to relax and enjoy yourself and come back refreshed. Try not to lose sight of the big picture. You are training to be a teacher so that you can live — not the other way round.

Do only what is necessary

It's the quality of work and the relevance of the work that counts, not the number of hours you spend on it. This doesn't mean you can cut corners or do the least you can get away with. Work out what is necessary to plan and deliver the lessons or write the essays properly and leave it at that. Do the necessary stuff first and don't allow yourself the luxury of delving into anything else just because it looks interesting. Just as in office work or running a home, you have to prioritize.

Don't let any of your work go to waste

Remember the filing cabinet. Whatever you have taught, you are bound to teach it again one day. All copies of lesson plans, medium- and long-term plans and the accompanying worksheets should be in a paper wallet clearly marked with the subject or Key Stage. Knowing where everything is, is vital because there is no point in keeping it if you have to spend ages looking for it.

Nor should you let what you have learned go to waste. Try to feed what you have learned back into your planning and practice in the classroom. It will give you a tremendous feeling of satisfaction to see that you have achieved that goal of putting theory into practice, and the feel-good factor helps to counteract stress.

Never work when you are tired

It is impossible to achieve anything worthwhile when you have a hammer banging away inside your head. All you will achieve is a headache and a lot of poor-quality 'work'. It is far better to go to bed and sleep, possibly getting up earlier the next morning and doing the work with a clear head.

Try to find out what is your optimal working period in the day. Some people function better in the early morning after a night's sleep when their head is clear. I know one student who, when writing her dissertation, regularly got up early when the house was quiet, and worked between 5am and 7am each morning. Some people get a 'second wind' late at night and after a strong cup of coffee can have two productive hours. It is important to know what your best period in the day is and capitalize by trying to do your most difficult work then.

Managing stress

If you realize you are suffering from stress, don't struggle along on your own. Talk to your partner, if you have one, and impress on him or her that you are just plain unable to cope with the current lifestyle and need help and support to get back to normal. If you are single, parents or friends may be your lifeline.

The student counselling service

Most universities have a student counselling service whose staff are accustomed to supporting students through the difficulties, so go along to see them. They may be able to give you advice on how to get yourself back on track.

Get medical help

If you start feeling a few of the symptoms mentioned above, the first step is to recognize that you are stressed and acknowledge that your health is more important than your studies, exams, lesson plans, keeping the house tidy and getting your dissertation in on time. Insisting on struggling on will make you much worse and put off your restoration to good health. If you are feeling weepy, snapping at people, unable to sleep and wanting to smoke or drink too much, go first to your supervisor or tutor or mentor and explain your work-related problems.

Then go straight to the doctor and tell him or her your symptoms and describe your hectic life. With a bit of luck, the doctor will write you off ill for a week, or two or three.

Treat the cause before the symptoms

You must also work out what is the cause of your stress and treat the cause, not the symptom. Look at the list of causes earlier in the chapter and ask yourself which apply to you. There will probably be more than one, or there may be others not mentioned. Try to pinpoint exactly what causes your stress and then you can start trying to work out how to get rid of it.

College work

If you cannot get through your college work in time, don't be afraid to ask your tutor for an extension, perhaps into the holidays to give you more time. This is not a sign of weakness. Many students do it every year, and lecturers much prefer you to give the work in later than crack up and not finish the course.

Sometimes students find the college work difficult to understand and are not confident to speak out in lectures and seminars to ask for explanations. I know a few who managed to overcome this with private tuition. It was costly but in the long run it was money well spent.

Sometimes students come out of exams, or even resits, fearing or knowing they have failed. The fear of telling their family, who are proud of them, becomes so large in their mind that they become stressed. There have been a few dreadfully distressing extreme cases where students have committed suicide, probably too wrapped up in their anxiety to realize that their sad death would cause infinitely more grief than their failure at university.

Needless to say, it is important for all students to recognize their importance in their parents' lives and to face up to telling them the facts. If you cannot do it face to face, telling them via a phone call, a letter or email is all right. Students must remember that their parents are not young and vulnerable. They are middle-aged and have had enough life experience to toughen them up to take life's little knocks. Most students find that their parents, though disappointed, are quite sympathetic and prepared to support them through the phase while they have time out, repeat the year or find a job.

School work

Some students (and teachers) are afraid to say that they cannot cope in case they look weak. This is unwise, because teachers always know if someone is not coping and they admire them less for pretending otherwise.

If you are finding it hard to cope in the school where you have your placement, look carefully at your timetable. Are you being asked to do more than the stipulated percentage of the timetable? Also, look at your individual classes. Have they given you a class (or two) that is difficult to manage, one that everyone hates? There is one in most schools and it is unfair to land it on a student unless they give you a lot of support. In either case, you must point this out to the head or head of department, whichever has the power to reduce your workload. Also, talk to your mentor and your college supervisor if you are not getting enough support.

Similarly, it may be that you have voluntarily taken on too much. Students and newly qualified teachers often do not realize how much the job involves until they are up to their ears in it. If you have taken on anything voluntarily and find you cannot cope, you will just have to say so and cut out the extra work.

If you have seen a doctor and are taking medication, make sure you tell the relevant people. It is now an offence to cause stress to people at work, and some employees have successfully sued their employer for it. Although you are not an employee, no one would want to be accused of causing anxiety to a student.

Accommodation problems

Living somewhere that is unpleasant or sharing with people with whom you cannot get on can add stress to a student's life. I have known students to sort that problem out by packing their bags and returning to the comfort of the family home. Of course, you can do that only if they live within convenient travelling distance of your college.

If they do not, then you must make an appointment to see whoever is in charge of student accommodation, tell him or her your problem and ask for help to find somewhere to live. Again say that your accommodation difficulties are causing you stress and that you have been to the doctor and are taking medication. To strengthen your case, make a list of times, dates and frequency of the problems you are experiencing. Being able to provide such a list makes sure you are taken seriously.

Family problems

Family problems can come in all shapes and sizes and at any time of your life. You can always get compassionate leave if there is a death in the family. A severe illness in the family can cause so much stress that students are unable to study. In cases like this, universities normally take a compassionate view and allow the student to take even a whole year off, to return home and resume their studies the following year.

Small children sometimes give their parents grief if they do not get enough attention because the parents are too preoccupied with their job or studies. You have got to impress on your partner that you need extra support, and if you are a single parent, this is where you must call on the support of the extended family. Don't try to be an island. That's what families are for − to look after each other. If there are no family members around, you may have to turn to friends to help you with childcare. Or if your doctor prescribes time off, you will be able to give your children a bit more care yourself for a while.

At this point, some young parents on teacher training begin to worry that although they like teaching, they may not be able to cope with it while childrearing. One option is to work part time after their induction year, and then build up to working full time as their children become more independent after a few years.

Now treat the symptoms

Even if you have taken some steps to remove the cause of your anxiety, you might still have that uncomfortable feeling of being tense and wound up. Many people have their own way of regaining that laid-back feeling.

Some find relief in attending a yoga class and practising the art of relaxation. Others find sitting quietly in a dark room listening to gentle classical music to be a relaxant. Exercise, too, brings back the feel-good factor. Many people enjoy an hour or two working out in the gym and others love to play a vigorous game of squash or badminton. Swimming is a great way to remove all of the tension from your body because you use most or all of your muscles, and some find the same effect if they go for a jog.

Those who are not sporty but still want some exercise in a pleasant, non-competitive atmosphere could try an evening class in some sort of lively dancing. Scottish, Irish and English country dancing all get the blood flowing more quickly.

Even a brisk walk at the end of a day's work helps you to feel better. Getting off the bus or train a stop early on the way home gets rid of the stress before you get there.

Don't forget the big picture
Always keep at the front of your mind the fact that your student days are short. Even three or four years is a very minor portion of your life. Remember that many students have suffered and eventually coped with the anxieties you are feeling now. This is a temporary phase and you will probably be so busy that each week will fly past you and when you finally walk onto the platform to receive your degree you will be wondering where the time has gone.

Balancing the course with family life

Teacher training is very demanding. Even if you are young and single and have no family commitments, it takes some perseverance to get through the course. If you have a partner and children, the task of coping with family life and your course becomes very complex. Your success as a parent and as a student is commensurate with your ability to balance the two roles.

What are the difficulties and how do you cope?

Quality time with the partner or the family
You will have much less time to spend with your partner or your family. Talk to your partner before you start. Make sure he or she understands that you will have a heavy workload, will not be able to

put the same amount of time and energy into your marriage or relationship until the course is over and that you will need support to get through it. Unless you have the wholehearted support of your partner, you are unlikely to stick it out to the end.

Children accept change better if the reasons for it are clear. Explain that you are going back to school and, like them, you will have homework and will not have quite so much time to spend enjoying their company. This has the benefit of setting the example that homework is important.

Tell them how long it will go on, if they are old enough to understand, because they like to know what's happening, and explain the advantage that when it finishes you will have a good job and much more money to spend on their birthday and Christmas presents, holidays and their maintenance at university. Children and teenagers are very open to promises of rewards and downright bribery.

With everyone in the family being pulled in every direction, it will be hard for you to find time to do things together, but it is worth trying, where possible, to have meals together. It is not until teenagers leave home and find themselves eating alone, filling themselves with junk food or the institutionalized meals of the refectory, that they appreciate the atmosphere of the cooked family meal at home.

Routine is also important. Children like to know where they stand: who is picking them up from school, looking after them, helping them with their homework. If you have someone different picking up your child from school, don't forget to tell the teacher as well as your child because some schools have a policy not to release the child otherwise. Having a similar routine each week reduces frustration for both you and your children.

Try to find some time in the weekend when you and your partner can spend time together doing something completely different. It helps you get things into perspective and remember that there is more to life than work and studying.

If you have children, it is also important to find time for them. Young children are more amenable to accepting less of your time if they know they are assured a regular time, such as Saturday afternoon, with you. It does not have to be expensive: a trip to the park or museum, or even quality time playing Monopoly if money is a problem.

The workload

As I have stressed, the course is intensive and the workload amounts to a full-time job. Some mature students find courses where the training is part time and so it is easier to combine it with running the home and bringing up the children, but of course it will last longer if done like this.

This is where the family comes in. You will already have warned your partner that you will have less time and need his or her support. Cut the housework to the bare minimum – dusting and vacuum-cleaning once a week, maximum.

Sit down with your partner and write down the tasks that are an absolute necessity: taking younger children to school and picking them up, laundering clothes, preparing meals. Decide who does each one and start a routine because jobs are then less likely to be left undone if they are delegated.

If you can afford it, get a domestic cleaner. Two hours once or twice a week can get the dusting, vacuuming and ironing done and take the strain off you both. Cleaners are not expensive and if you ask around, you can usually find one. If you cannot find one, an advertisement in a shop 'nosy board' or local library usually brings several replies.

Ask your older children to help by taking on little jobs around the house, according to their age and ability. As long as they are not up to their ears in studying for GCSEs or worse, they are often quite amenable. Taking responsibility and being shown proper appreciation for it gives them self-esteem and I found that offering extra pocket money for chores around the home always worked.

Having a baby while at college

A very small number of student teachers become pregnant while still at college. This makes life very difficult because it creates a great many logistical difficulties. Even if you are a male student, you need to plan your family carefully, because a birth during the exam period could mean the difference between passing and failing, given the chances of sleep loss. It is best to try to avoid pregnancy, because it is far from easy.

Few colleges have crèches and you may not be able to afford a child minder, so if you are a new mother, you may have to take your baby into college with you and hope the baby stays silent or sleeps through lectures.

The main problem – loss of sleep – can make studying and absorbing anything during lectures really difficult.

One of my colleagues, a successful student, teacher and mother, coped by turning up for college each day to get her attendance mark, sitting through the lectures with her baby strapped to her and her Dictaphone on so that she could listen to the lecture later, at home, when the baby was in bed. If you try this, it would be wise to sit near the door to make a quick getaway if the baby howls.

I have known a few people cope with it, but pregnancy during teacher training is not practical.

Childcare

Finding reliable childcare is the most common problem in families where both parents go out to work or study. Of course, having a full-time nanny is ideal but most couples cannot afford one, especially if one parent is a student. Sometimes two families get together and share a nanny to make it more affordable. Others solve the problem by having an au pair, but if you haven't got a spare bedroom, that's not possible.

Some young parents are in the happy position of having nearby grandparents to mind the baby or take the children to school or nursery and pick them up. Grandparents can be wonderful. They are less likely than babysitters to complain if you change arrangements or if you are late, and you can go to college secure in the knowledge that your child is being treated with loving care. However, it is unlikely that they will want the job of minding your children full time and so you will need to negotiate carefully with them, as they have lives and interests too. One day per week seems fairly reasonable. Their goodwill will last longer if you do not take advantage of them.

Finding a child minder

If your children are too young to go to nursery, then you will have to find a child minder. Local councils keep a list but, of course, you will prefer personal recommendation.

When you first visit, it is best to take your baby with you to see how they respond to each other. I would also go during a working day so that you could see what other children she (or he) minds and decide whether you are happy with your child being with her. Some parents will only leave their child with a minder who takes no others, but I always liked there to be other children so that mine could become accustomed to the company.

You will probably use your own intuition to judge whether it is a happy, caring home, but you must also note whether the home looks clean and safe and whether there is cigarette smoke in the atmosphere. Ask questions about the daily routine; some child minders take their children to the local parent and baby group and some to the local gym or swimming pool when they have a parent and toddler session.

It is best to check that the child minder is registered with the local council and ask to see the latest inspection report. Child minders are inspected by Ofsted as well. Ask for the names and telephone numbers of past parents so that you can contact them to take up references.

If you advertise, you might be lucky and find a young parent who is willing to bring his or her child to your home and look after them both together. This will be more expensive but a lot more convenient and your child will have the comfort of having his or her own toys around all day and will not have to suffer the discomfort of being taken out in the cold in winter. If you are in this fortunate position, don't forget to check that the minder is registered with the local council.

Separation during teaching practice

You could be very unfortunate and have one of your teaching practice placements away from home so you see the family only at the weekend, when you are tired and have work to do.

As soon as you get settled into the course, find out who is in charge of organizing the teaching practice placements and approach them to explain that you have children and would be grateful to be placed in a school within easy travelling distance of home. Lecturers have told me that they try to be amenable about such requests.

Travelling

Travelling can be tiring and time-consuming. It is important to take a course as close to home as you can manage. You still need to study the course in detail to make sure it is what you want, and this can lead to your balancing the course you might prefer against the one that will save you ten hours of travelling time each week.

Making technology work for you

Today's technology is a godsend to households where both parents are working. Most areas in the UK have a delivery service from a nearby supermarket. Shopping online can save you hours of tedious supermarket shelf wandering. Most of them show the bargains on the screen so you don't lose out, and the delivery charge is not a waste of money because you will save litres of petrol by eliminating the journey. It's also a great time-saver when you are buying Christmas, birthday and wedding presents.

Microwaves are another boon. Your teenage children will not

always be able to make it on time for every meal. In fact, teenagers, on principle, have to be different to demonstrate their growing maturity. They will appreciate being able to reheat their evening meal in two minutes and you will not suffer the irritation of watching a nutritious meal being spoilt by being left in the oven for an hour or two.

A freezer saves you time. You can cook in bulk at the weekend and use the microwave to reheat it during the week. It doesn't spoil the taste if done properly. In fact, some meals, such as curries, improve in taste. Buying in bulk and storing in the freezer also saves time spent shopping, and saves money.

If you can afford a dishwasher, it will also save time, especially if loading it and unloading it could be the children's job.

Exam time

There can be no doubt that performance in exams, in fact in anything, is enhanced by an alert state of mind. You should make sure your children understand that you must be in bed early, even if it means going to bed before your older children. This has the added advantage that it sets them an example. They will take you more seriously if you have been seen to practise what you have preached to them.

Enlist your children's sympathy. If they have done a few exams themselves, you can appeal to their good nature with comments such as 'You know what it's like, dear. I just have to concentrate on them to make sure I pass.' If they are too young to understand, try 'It's only for a short time until my exams are over.' Then promise a fun day out when the exams are finished.

If tiredness prevents you from studying, get your partner to keep the children quiet or take them out on a Saturday or Sunday afternoon while you go to bed. There is nothing like a sleep in the afternoon to set you up for a productive evening.

Here are a few tips to get through the exams:

- Ask the cleaner to do a few extra hours during the exam period.
- If there is a school holiday in the weeks before the exams, ask around the extended family whether some kind aunt, uncle or grandparents would have your children for a few days' 'holiday'.
- It is better to study in the library if there are too many distractions at home.
- Make it clear to your family that you cannot be asked to do anything extra for them until the exams are over.
- Never skimp on food. Proper, nutritious meals keep your energy

levels up and stop you becoming ill when you are under pressure. Try to get your partner or older children to do the cooking. Failing that, only have meals that need only a short preparation time, or buy some fish and chips or some other kind of takeaway if you can afford it.

♦ Keep your vitamin C levels and omega oil levels up to stay healthy.

♦ Stress can cause headaches. Keep the painkillers handy, and drink plenty of water because stress dehydrates.

♦ If your children are stroppy, let your partner handle it.

Preparing for the exams

♦ Sit down with your friends at college and look at some old exam papers. Some people are clever at spotting topics that come up regularly.

♦ Share the load. Sometimes students get together and study different parts of the syllabus and share their notes. Of course, you can do this only with people you can trust.

♦ Try out an old exam paper under exam conditions. Your tutor might be willing to read your answers and offer some advice.

Money problems

If you have given up a job to do the course, this will mean a cut in your weekly budget. It is best to sit down with your partner and work out how much less money you will have and how you will downsize your budget to cope with the shortfall. Sometimes this means cutting out holidays, trips to the cinema and theatre, and meals at restaurants.

Try not to make the mistake of skimping on food. It's a very false economy because it reduces your ability to cope and you are more likely to become ill.

At the weekend it is tempting to think you cannot go anywhere or do anything because you are short of cash. In fact, there are lots of things you can do that do not cost money. A trip to the local park to play on the swings and roundabouts, or a game of football or cricket with their dad, is just as much fun to children as a trip to the cinema and costs nothing.

Even if you cannot afford aeroplane fares and hotels abroad, you may still be able to afford holidays. There are plenty of places in Britain with campsites. Children love camping because it seems like an adventure to them. You don't have to spoil it for yourself by doing lots of shopping and cooking. There are often cafés close by, or you can resort to fish and chips or takeaways.

Don't forget that there is some financial help for students. Look at the advice given on funding in Chapter 1 or visit the website www.tda.gov.uk/Recruit/thetrainingprocess/fundinginengland.aspx for up-to-date information.

Keeping your sanity

Keep reminding yourself that the situation is temporary. Most people in this situation say the advantages far outweigh the drawbacks. When you are qualified, you will still have to work hard, but you will have more money and you will not have to cope with the strain of exams and being permanently judged, and you will feel more secure.

There will probably be other mature students on the course who have children. Make friends with them and you can encourage and support each other. You might be able to team up with them during the school holidays. A trip to the local swimming pool or pantomime is more fun when you share it with another family.

Take time out at the end of each term to enjoy the company of other students. There is usually a party or a meal out at the end of each term, or the occasional night in the pub during the term. Try not to rush home quickly to the family every night because a change can be as beneficial as a rest and you deserve it now and again.

When it's over

Now is the time to reward yourself and your family. Have a family treat such as a special night out, a visit to a theme park or a weekend away. Make it clear to your children that you appreciated their support while you were doing the course and this is to reward them for helping you through it.

Once the prospect of a larger income is secure, you can sit down with your partner and enjoy the luxury of being able to plan how to improve the quality of life for your family.

5 | Getting ready for the real world

Finding your first job

Finding your first job is an inescapable hurdle and one not to be underestimated, but it is quite an exciting task. After the long years of study, students feel they are finally about to reach their goal. Sometimes students are so keen that they apply for lots of jobs and excitedly take the first one offered. This can lead to disaster if they take an unsuitable post in a school that is desperate to fill its vacancies. It is particularly important that you find a post in a school where you can fit in and feel comfortable.

Beware of market forces. In times of extreme surplus, highly qualified teachers with top grades in their teaching practices are turned down by dozens of schools, frequently without an acknowledgement. In times of shortage, teachers are given expenses to attend interviews and offered a choice of schools.

At the present time, 2008, we are in a period of shortage in some areas of the state sector, especially in some subjects such as maths and science in secondary schools. If you can offer either of these subjects, you will be shortlisted for every post for which you apply, and quickly snapped up. You may well have the added bonus of about one-tenth of your student loan being wiped out for each year in which you work in a maintained school. There is also a teacher shortage in some parts of the country, especially the inner cities.

Rising and falling birth rates can have an effect on the number of jobs available. For example, in Northern Ireland the birth rate has fallen so dramatically that newly qualified teachers (NQTs) rarely get a job when they leave university and for their first year or two have to take any supply work that is available. If you are doing the one-year postgraduate course, you might take this into consideration, but if you are doing a three- or four-year course you can ignore it because things will be different by the time you finish. On the whole, teaching is more slump-proof than most professions, because people keep having children regardless. It is also a fairly secure job.

Competition for jobs varies in different parts of the country and different types of school. A peaceful prep school can have 30 or more applications for a job, while a school on a council estate a mile away can have one or two. If you want to find out where there are most jobs available, browse the TES jobs line (www.tes.co.uk) in the first month of each term, when most new jobs are advertised, and you can also sign up for daily or weekly email alerts for posts meeting your own particular criteria.

Some students are afraid to apply for jobs in schools that are challenging. Some are deterred by the labels 'special measures' or 'fresh start', or by finding that the school has a high proportion of pupils who are in the early stages of learning English. High levels of poverty that impact on pupils' learning also deter some students. Before rejecting schools of this type, I would suggest a visit, looking closely at the way in which the staff and pupils interact and how the head leads his or her team. I have spent many happy and satisfying years in challenging inner-city schools and have often found that the mutually supportive staff and happy atmosphere made up for many difficulties. Also, you will learn quickly in such schools and acquire skills that will give you confidence to face anything. A few successful years in a challenging school will also help you onto the shortlist when you apply for promotion.

In some parts of the UK, government policy has more influence on the availability of jobs than the birth rate does. In recent decades, education has fluctuated up and down various governments' lists of priorities.

The economy of the country is perhaps the greatest influence. If the money is not made available, the jobs disappear. Also, in times when graduates are being made redundant from industry, they turn to teaching, which is seen as a safe alternative. This is easy for some because they may have trained as teachers before changing their minds and going off to work elsewhere. Teaching has the advantage that in a recession it is a fairly secure job and in prosperous times there is a greater choice of jobs available.

What to consider

Decide on an area of the country where you would ideally like to live. If you are married and/or have children, this is probably already decided for you.

Keep an open mind on the type of school: state, independent, inner city or affluent suburb, challenging failed school, satisfactory or outstanding successful school. You can have a happy or an unhappy experience in any of these. Of course, some are easier to get jobs in than others.

Even in these secular days your religion can count. If you are an Anglican, Roman Catholic or Jew, or even a lapsed member of a particular faith, you have a much better chance of finding a job in a school of your chosen (or rejected) faith.

Occasionally you can use whom you know, as well as what you know. Of course, you can never openly canvass, but if you have a friend or relation who knows of a school that is looking for a teacher, a quiet word of recommendation can help. Some senior members of staff have told me they try to employ teachers who have been recommended by someone personally known to them.

Do not feel disadvantaged by your youth or inexperience. Both of these are huge points in your favour. Newly qualified teachers are obviously cheaper. Many heads prefer newly qualified teachers because they can save money to redirect towards equipment, books or supply cover. For a head, your inexperience is an added bonus because it is easier to mould a novice into the school's own way of working. An experienced teacher, especially one who has plenty of faith in him- or herself, is sometimes seen as a threat by the head who has not spent much time with a class of kids for years, has lost the knack and feels out of touch.

By far the easiest thing is to find a job in the school where you have done your final teaching practice. Of course, this is not always practical because you may not want to stay in the area, but either way it is worth cultivating the approval of the headteacher, head of department or even class teacher, because you'll need someone who has seen you in operation to write your reference.

If you are unattached to either a partner or a part of the country, and are prepared to go anywhere, one good insurance policy is to find out an area of teacher shortage and apply to that education authority. I acquired my first post after a five-minute interview of uncomplicated questioning in the Inner London Education Authority during the dire shortage in the early 1970s.

At that time, it was practically impossible for a single person to survive on an NQT's salary, and teachers were leaving in droves. Schools could rarely find a teacher for every post, and so were accepting almost everyone who applied as well as funding their intercity train and even plane fares, and giving them an allowance towards a day's meals on the day of the interview. The laws of supply and demand are a wonderful thing!

Today, some schools are finding it so difficult that they are recruiting from abroad. Some teachers' agencies will set up interviews for headteachers on the telephone to teachers in Australia.

Choosing the right school

Choosing the right school is vitally important to passing your induction year. In the past, some newly qualified teachers have spent a miserable first year through not researching the school first to make sure it was the right school for them.

There are lots of things to check out, most of which can only be done when you visit the school. However, before you go, you can do some advance preparation by checking out the following.

The Investors in People award

Investors in People is a prestigious award conferred on schools and other places of work after they have been rigorously inspected. An establishment seeking the award has to prove that it treats its staff at all levels with care, and provide them with opportunities to progress and develop their skills to benefit their own careers as well as the place of work.

If you apply to a school that bears the award, it is a sign that the staff are appreciated and treated with respect.

The school's last Ofsted report

Every state school in the country is inspected about once every three years by Her Majesty's Office for Standards in Education (Ofsted). Independent schools are inspected every six years, sometimes by the Independent Schools Inspectorate (ISI). The inspectors inspect the paperwork, and some lessons have to be observed during the week. They look at a full set of books from a pupil respectively in the bottom, middle and top of each ability group in each year group. In recent years the focus of the inspection has shifted towards the senior management team more than the class teacher. This takes the pressure off the class teachers, some of whom may not have even one lesson observed.

Independent schools can be given several months' notice of an inspection, whereas state schools are given only two or three days' notice. In both cases there can be a frenzy of activity before the inspectors appear. A few teachers enjoy the cut and thrust of it, but the majority loathe it. For some, the judgemental aspect gets the whole thing off on the wrong foot because even the most competent teachers have the occasional lesson that goes badly, and the thought of one such lesson being observed and classified as 'poor' is unnerving to teachers, most of whom care deeply about their credibility.

Every school's most recent general inspection report from Ofsted has been published on the internet (www.ofsted.gov.uk). It is worth reading it to get an overall picture of the school. If the report is more than two years old, bear in mind that the school may have changed since its inspection date, especially if there is a new headteacher. It is sensible to check before you apply to the school, just so that you are aware of the date of the next inspection.

Going into a school that has recently had an unfavourable Ofsted report is attractive to those who are stimulated by a challenge, thrive on pressure and do not value a peaceful life. There is, of course, the advantage that a new teacher is untainted by the failed inspection, since he or she cannot possibly be blamed for events that took place before his or her time. Another advantage is that it is easy to find a job in a failed school, although parents and governors will be looking to new teachers with a positive attitude and lots of energy to make substantial improvements. They will expect new teachers to inject the children with the enthusiasm that they may have lacked in the past. You can always look on the bright side: once the school has hit the bottom, its only direction is up.

The headteacher

Check whether the same head is *in situ*, because a change of head is the greatest single factor in radical change. Never expect a school to be the same when the head changes. Experienced teachers will tell you they have known schools to change out of all recognition, for good or for ill, in the two years after a new head came.

Inside information

It helps if you know someone on the inside. Do you know anyone who has done a teaching practice there, worked there, or sent their own children there? Only listen to information that is recent, because in these fast-moving times the whole ethos and atmosphere of a school can change with alarming speed. Also, remember that there will be a certain amount of subjectivity in people's comments because every school has its share of staff, pupils and parents who are less content than others.

Know the target

It is usually worth consulting the local league tables, but view them with caution. Schools in wealthy areas with supportive, professional parents should be high up the league. In a school in an impoverished area with large numbers of pupils who do not speak much English, and high mobility of homeless families, it is much more difficult to raise standards and keep them high. If the former type of school is halfway down the table, it is not particularly successful. If the latter is halfway up, it is doing a superb job.

Do not be deterred from working in the latter type. My experience of children who suffer extremes of poverty is that they enjoy coming to school to have something interesting to do. They are frequently willing to work and can be grateful for your efforts, particularly if they cannot speak much English. Recent arrivals in the UK are usually desperate to learn English because they cannot make friends or feel accepted until they do.

Also, the staff in this type of school tend to be supportive of each other and so there is often a happy atmosphere in the staffroom. The parents may be unable to support your efforts, but then, they won't be pushy and pressurizing about their children's progress and where they come in the ranking order of the class.

You may, however, have to cope with a certain amount of aggression from some parents who are resentful of schools in general, sometimes because their own experiences of school were unhappy or unsuccessful, or because they have a problem with any kind of authority figure.

In schools in very affluent areas, you may have aggression from demanding, pushy, even snooty, parents who think they know it all. In independent schools you will find parents less willing to accept your judgement. They often have the attitude that because they are paying for their children's education, that gives them the automatic right to tell you what to do.

Filling in the form and writing the letter of application

Remember that the head's first impression of you is important, so make it a good one. Give as much information as you can about your previous experience of working with children or teenagers, making sure you get the dates right. Never write straight onto the form. I always make at least one photocopy of the form first and practise on that before filling in the form itself, which, of course, has to be as neat as you can make it.

This is most important as heads make their decisions on whether to short-list partly on the basis of the letter. Since this is your first job, you will not be expected to write a very long letter; one or two sides of A4 paper is plenty. Unless the advertisement states otherwise, always type it. Choose the lecturer with whom you have the best working relationship and ask him or her to be your referee, and ditto for the teacher with whom you had the best relationship on teaching practice for your second referee.

Before you start

Ring up the school and ask them to send you an application form, a school prospectus and a job description and look closely at the details of all three. Every point on the job description must be covered in your letter of application. Make a list of all the points and decide where in the letter you will put each one. Your list might look like this.

1. able to work amicably in a team
2. able to cope with wide range of abilities
3. sympathetic towards underprivileged pupils
4. knowledgeable about my subject
5. having a positive approach to discipline
6. willing to take part in educational visits and school journey
7. able to use ICT across the curriculum
8. able to challenge and stretch bright pupils

Getting the tone right

Write your statement out roughly and redraft it, checking all the points below before adding the final one to the application form.

The tone is as important as the content. Remember, the head might have lots of applicants to choose from, and will choose one who sounds enthusiastic over one who sounds matter-of-fact. You must sound eager as well as serious about the value of the job. Use expressions such as:

'I enjoyed my experience as ...'
'I experienced great satisfaction in learning ...'
'I learned a great deal about the value of ...'
'It has been a privilege to work/study in ...'
'This is the kind of school where I can contribute a lot ...'
'It is my goal to make a real difference ...'

Content and structure

First paragraph
Start with an introductory sentence stating the post for which you are

applying and any reference mentioned in the advertisement. Say which college or university faculty you are studying in at present.

Second paragraph
Try using these points:

◆ Why you are especially interested in working in that school – you like its ethos; you have read its last Ofsted report and were impressed.
◆ If it is well up the league tables, say you think it would be 'challenging' (heads like that word) to work in a school with high standards.
◆ If the school is not high in the league tables, say that you have a special interest in giving opportunity to children who are not advantaged.
◆ Make sure you address every point that is mentioned in the advertisement. Some heads go through letters with a list, ticking them off as they read them.

Third paragraph
◆ Tell them about your particular academic strengths and interests, preferably ones that are sought in the advertisement.
◆ Write about your extra-curricular activities which you can put to good use in the school – football, cricket, any form of music, art or drama, any Combined Cadet Force or adventure type of activity. Heads love teachers who offer extra skills and activities.
◆ Tell them about your summer jobs or any previous experience of working with children or teenagers and how they have given you useful skills such as organization ability, ability to handle responsibility and being in a position of authority, ability to work amicably in a team.

Final paragraph
Add the names of your referees and finish with a sentence such as 'I should view this post as an interesting/stimulating challenge' or 'This post would be a valuable opportunity for me to extend my own learning/development/expertise in ...'

The unofficial interview
If it is a state school, always telephone and ask to come and see the school. Most heads want to meet applicants before the interview and

many are sizing them up in preparation for short-listing. The impression you make at this point is as important as the formal interview. Some heads who have lots of applicants will tell you to wait until the day of the interview, but I have not yet met a state-school head who will short-list a teacher who has not at least asked for a visit.

Private-school heads take a different stance and will short-list purely on the basis of the application form or CV and the letter of application, and do not normally allow you to visit until the day of the interview.

Look and act the part

Always power-dress for the preliminary visit and the interview, whatever you intend wearing for the rest of your life. For men, if not a suit, at least smart trousers and jacket, shirt and tie. Women should wear a suit or smart dress and carry a spare pair of tights in their handbag. If you are going on public transport in heavy rain, a change of shoes would be worth the bother.

Make sure you know the names of the head and, possibly, the deputy and/or head of department, and use them. They like that, and it creates a good impression. Try to arrive 15 minutes early if you can, but never late. Punctuality is extremely important for teachers. Walk in with your head up, look the head in the eye and smile confidently.

What to look for

Always visit during the school day to see what the school is really like, because every school looks remarkably peaceful after the pupils go home. While the head is sizing you up, you must look out for and give thought to as many of the following aspects as you can.

The headteacher

The head is the greatest single factor influencing any school. Heads set the tone for the school and most of the attitudes and behaviour of the staff can be traced back to him or her.

Is the head friendly and approachable and do you feel comfortable in his or her presence? Does he or she seem interested in you? Would you feel comfortable talking to the head if you were in difficulty? These considerations are more important in a small school, where you will have more direct contact with the head. In a larger school you will have more contact with heads of department than with the headteacher.

As you walk around the school, notice whether the head speaks pleasantly to the pupils, teachers and other staff. Does he or she allow the staff to use his or her first name? Nowadays only an older head would still expect to be addressed as Mr, Mrs or Miss – except in front of the pupils, of course.

The staff

◆ *Atmosphere*. Try to assess whether the school has a happy, welcoming atmosphere. Do the staff look as if they get on well together and enjoy their work? For me, this is more important than a high place on the league tables.

◆ *Staff* in situ. Are the other teachers people to whom you can relate? Are there kindred spirits here? Will they help you through the induction year? I know one young teacher who spent her first year in a school where everyone was at least 20 years older than her. Although everyone was kind to her, she often felt lonely and isolated. Some teachers suggest that the male/female ratio can affect the atmosphere.

◆ *Staff turnover*. Ask what the annual rate of staff turnover is. A low percentage rate is an encouraging sign because, unless there is a shortage of jobs, teachers will not stay in a school if it is not a pleasant, happy place. If the turnover is high, the head may resent your asking, but this is unlikely to matter because it is probably not a school where you would want to work anyway.

Pupils

◆ *In the classroom*. Are the pupils on task, polite and reasonably interested in their work?

◆ *In the corridors*. Does their standard of behaviour slip as soon as they walk out of the structured environment of the classroom?

◆ *Playground behaviour*. Try to see whether there are any fights in the playground. I would consider a harmonious playground a higher priority than good SATs or GCSE results, although it is of course worth looking at those as well.

◆ *Out of school – in the street, at bus stops, in the buses (secondary)*. I think pupils' true selves appear when they are completely unsupervised.

◆ *Noise levels*. Check the noise levels in classrooms. Is it a noise of positive activity or just plain rowdy?

◆ *Behaviour policy*. As you walk around a primary school, look out for charts with children's names, stars and stickers. Ask the head what incentive schemes and reward systems the school uses. It is sensible for a school to have a few positive ways of encouraging children, but if they have lots of them, tread carefully because that usually means that the children are difficult to motivate and there are difficulties with behaviour management. In a secondary school, notice whether there is an honours board or any other noticeboard with information or newspaper clippings concerning pupils' achievements. Is there a display cabinet with cups, trophies or shields? These are always a positive sign. And, of course, don't forget to admire them.

The job

◆ *Pupil–teacher relationships.* How do pupils and teachers interact? In harmony or confrontationally?

◆ *The styles of teaching.* Are they conventional, progressive, practical, creative, boring? Is there much freedom of teaching style, is it prescribed and is it a format into which you can fit comfortably?

◆ *What the job demands.* Remember, interviews are a two-way process. Teachers often forget that they need to assess whether the school is right for them. A helpful headteacher will try to give you plenty of information about everything that the job requires. Don't be afraid to ask questions. In fact, have a few questions ready to ask.

◆ *The extra clauses.* Check what overnight school journeys you will have to go on, and whether there are any Saturday commitments.

The ethos of the school

If the school has to cater for a wide range of races, classes and creeds, it is a definite point in the school's favour if pupils of all the races mix harmoniously. This can be achieved only in an atmosphere of tolerance and mutual respect. It is impossible in a short visit to gauge this fully, but you might notice the following:

◆ Is the multiracial aspect of the school population reflected in the displays?

◆ Are Muslim girls and Sikh boys allowed to wear veils and patkas respectively – a small gauge of the school's ethos of tolerance?

◆ Does the artwork reflect each culture?

◆ Is there music from different cultures?

◆ Does the racial mix of the staff differ greatly from that of the pupils or are there some teachers or non-teaching staff who can speak the language of some of the pupils? (This point must be viewed cautiously, as many schools try hard but are unable to find suitable staff with the right mother tongue.)

◆ In a multiracial school, is there a policy that English is the only language allowed? Are pupils allowed to speak their own language among themselves or, more importantly, are bilingual pupils encouraged to interpret for new pupils who are still in the process of learning English?

The practical everyday issues

◆ *Parking space.* Don't underestimate its importance. You could find yourself in an inner-city school with no on-site or street parking and so you would have to use public transport. If that is the case, check whether the journey is convenient.

◆ *Name policy.* Never address the head by his or her first name until you are sure it is the acceptable thing to do. In a few schools the staff are still not allowed to do so. In others, the children address the staff, even the head, by their first names. This can be important to some teachers who have strong feelings on the subject.

◆ *Lunch-time arrangements.* Are the staff expected to eat in the dining hall with the pupils and the noise? It can give you a headache after a frustrating morning and leave you less fit for the afternoon's challenges. Do they give you a free lunch if you eat there? Is the food edible? This is not a trivial issue. A nutritious midday meal and a break are important to many teachers so they can be on form in the afternoon.

◆ *The dress code.* In many schools, men have to wear a smart shirt and tie. Muslim women teachers especially need to check whether it is acceptable to wear a veil if they wish to do so. You could avoid the problem by showing up for the interviews wearing what is right for you as there would be no point in making a fuss after you had been appointed. If you make it clear you will be wearing your traditional dress to work, they will employ you only if they find that acceptable. Who would want to work in an atmosphere of intolerance anyway?

◆ *Religious holidays.* If you will want to have time off for Jewish or Muslim festivals, for example, it is best to ask before you are appointed, as it can cause grief if you leave it until close to the event and are refused. A good time to ask is when you are offered a post. Also, if you are Jewish and need to leave school before sundown on Fridays, tell the head about that in advance. Of course, you can soften it by saying something like 'I am happy to do anything after school Monday to Thursday, but on Fridays I do need to leave promptly.'

The official interview and lesson observation

After reading the application forms and meeting candidates, the head and governors select a short list for interviewing formally and observing a short prepared lesson.

The lesson

Many schools ask teachers to do a brief sample lesson before they are interviewed. If this is the case for you, get it right. Many applicants feel nervous doing it for the first time, but there is nothing to worry about, because heads normally give candidates a fairly manageable class, and the pupils are unlikely to misbehave because the headteacher is in the room observing them as well as the nervous candidate.

In some secondary schools, after the candidate has left the classroom the pupils are asked to give their opinions and vote on whether they would like him or her to be appointed. Although the pupils do not make the final decision, their views, if canvassed, must be taken into consideration and could make the difference if the interview was mediocre.

You will be told in advance what age group and what subject you will be faced with. You may have to deliver a complete lesson or it just might be a mental and oral starter. You may be given a complete class or you may have just a group. I have known all of these to happen.

You may be given free rein to choose a topic or you may be given a specific objective.

Make sure you check:

◆ the pupils' level of attainment
◆ whether the group is mixed-ability or streamed
◆ what the pupils have already studied in that particular topic, because you don't want to produce a lesson on something they have already done
◆ what resources are available: books, maths equipment
◆ what the exact length of the lesson is; if applicable, whether there will be an assistant present

Write a lesson plan with timings on it for each part of the lesson. If an IWB is available, put a resource on a memory stick, but make sure in advance that this is acceptable.

Tips for the lesson

They are looking for something interesting delivered in an enthusiastic manner.

◆ Keep smiling and speak in a calm, pleasant manner.

◆ Write your objective on the board before you start, and make sure the pupils understand what it means.

◆ In your starter, ask questions to draw information from the pupils.

◆ Whatever task or activity you have planned, make sure you have all your resources at hand and in the right order.

◆ If you are going to use the IWB, make sure you have a back-up plan in case the technology fails.

◆ If the class is of mixed ability, make sure you have work that is differentiated – something to simplify the task for the less able and an extra challenge for the most able.

◆ In your plenary, ask pupils to give explanations on the content of the lesson.

◆ Make sure you finish the lesson on time. Finish by referring back to the objective on the board. Ask a pupil to explain what he or she has learned. A good finishing line is 'That's a perfect explanation and a perfect place to end. Well done, everyone.'

The interview

Remember that interviews are a two-way process: you are finding out about the job as much as they are finding out about you. Everyone has their own priority. Mine is to ensure that the head and teachers are people whom I feel I can trust and work with amicably.

It is not enough to give the right answers; they also want teachers who are pleasant company and can form satisfactory relationships with adults and children. They know you are inexperienced but will probably allow for that if you show enthusiasm and commitment to your career.

If you are applying for a secondary post, it is essential to study the National Curriculum document for your subject(s) as they will be eager to know whether your knowledge and understanding are sound. If the post is in a primary school, they will focus on the curricula for the age group with which you will be working, so an hour or two reminding yourself of its content is time well spent.

You can expect to be asked at least some of the questions listed below, so it is wise to smooth the path for yourself by writing short essay-type answers once you have been short-listed. The night before your interview, ask a friend to read your questions to give you a practice interview. Read your answers about an hour before the interview to refresh your memory.

The questions will vary depending on the type of school and the needs of the children. Sometimes questions are designed to find out how you would cope in certain circumstances. Often an NQT cannot possibly know exactly what to do because they do not have the required experience, but it is important that you show the confidence and common sense to seek advice and guidance and are willing to learn. So don't worry if you do not always have the perfect answer for every situation.

Likely questions and a few suggested answers

Primary

Q 'How would you organize your class?'

A Prepare some notes explaining how you would organize the class for different subjects, emphasizing the need for variety according to the needs of the children and the demands of the subject.

Describe how you would have a system for giving pupils responsibility for looking after books and equipment and keeping areas of the classroom tidy. Tell them how you would have differentiated ability groups for maths, and mixed groups for practical subjects like science and PE, especially if there are pupils in the early stages of learning English.

Q 'How would you set up your classroom?'

A You can start by saying that you are acutely aware that the environment has a strong effect on behaviour. Your aim would be to make the classroom an attractive, stimulating place with colourful displays of pupils' work to encourage them, and show that teachers consider their achievements important.

Also point out that convenience reduces frustration and so equipment should be accessible to the pupils, who should be trained to put everything in its place, preferably labelled, when not in use. Say you are aware of the importance of pupils being seated where they can comfortably see the board or interactive whiteboard.

Add a comment about the need to seat pupils with others with whom they can work amicably.

Q 'How would you extend the more able and support the less able?'

A Make it clear you are aware of the wide difference in pupils' abilities, and levels of English if it is a multicultural school, and hence the need for differentiation of work: extension work for the more able, simplified work for the less able. Point out that a large part of helping pupils to achieve is tied up with making the lessons fun and building up their confidence and self-belief. There are plenty of maths games on the market for pupils of all abilities, to make the subject enjoyable and give lots of extra practice at each level to enable them to acquire concepts painlessly. There are also lots of sets of books of short play scripts that pupils of different levels can enjoy reading in parts together.

Add that a large part of getting the best out of pupils of all levels is making the subject real. The best way to do this is to back up the Literacy Hour with an occasional educational trip. There is nothing like seeing a film or theatre production of a play or novel to make the print come off the page and enthral the reluctant reader. A trip to a historical site with 'hands-on' activities always raises the enthusiasm levels and the quality of writing produced after the event.

Q   'How do you view the role of the nursery nurse/the classroom assistant?' (Infants)

A   You could explain that nursery nurses have proper training for the post so they must be given trust and responsibility that matches their qualification and skills. They should be included in the planning and delivery of the curriculum. A teacher should find out what the nursery nurse's skills are and make best use of them. Also, as professionals, nursery nurses have to grow and develop like everyone else. They must be given opportunities to go on courses and learn new skills, and to use the training for the pupils' benefit.

Teaching assistants (TAs) vary enormously. Some have very few qualifications and some have degrees. Some have completed courses and achieved Higher Level Teaching Assistant status. Others, such as learning support assistants (LSAs), have also completed courses of training and are invaluable for supporting children with special needs. As time has passed, they have been given more responsibility. Say that you believe it is important to use their skills for teaching groups within the class and that they should be encouraged to extend their skills by going on courses, and be given more opportunities within the classroom. They should not be expected to plan lessons on their own or left alone with the class to teach a lesson, unless they have enough training and experience and are agreeable to taking on that amount of responsibility. Add that you would like to know the school's policy for delegating responsibility to TAs and LSAs.

Q   'How would you set about supporting pupils in your lessons who spoke very little or no English?'

A   If you speak the language of any of the pupils, for example Urdu or Cantonese, you are at great advantage. Say that you would start by consulting the EAL teacher for advice about what they can do and by reading the pupils' EAL records. Emphasize the value of mother-tongue teaching. Ask whether they have any mother-tongue teachers or assistants, or any bilingual texts in the school. These ideas should help:

◆   In Key Stage 1, allow the pupil lots of opportunities to indulge in imaginative play, as infants pick up language very quickly.

◆   Start each lesson by explaining the keywords for the lesson. (Doing so also helps some of the English-speaking pupils.)

◆   As far as possible, put pupils who are in the early stages of learning English next to bilingual pupils who can translate for them, and encourage the bilinguals to support their classmates.

◆   Similarly, if it is difficult or impossible for them to grasp new concepts with unfamiliar language, for example in maths, it is fair practice to ask a capable bilingual pupil to explain work in the child's mother tongue.

◆   Always organize the timetable so that they have practical lessons like science and technology when the EAL support teacher is in the classroom to support them.

◆   Involve them in collaborative tasks where they will work with English-speaking pupils who can be good role models for them.

◆   Give them the opportunity to access the same lessons as the rest of the class by simplifying the worksheets to their level. EAL pupils learn better in practical lessons.

◆   Build into lessons opportunities to practise speaking.

◆   When EAL pupils start to read, they need a lot of practice, so it works well to ask competent readers in the class to listen to them reading for five or ten minutes each day.

Secondary

Q   'Give an example of how you have got pupils interested and excited about your subject.'

A   Say you believe that pupils are best excited by giving them lessons that are fun. Point out how school trips can raise the interest level and make a subject come alive. Pupils almost always produce a better quality of work after a day trip.

Pupils also prefer subjects that are relevant to their lives. It is always worthwhile showing pupils areas in their lives in which they can use the information or skill.

Variety is the spice of life. Use visual, auditory and kinaesthetic methods. Pupils love hands-on activities. Put in a few examples that are appropriate to your subject. Try to present work in a variety of ways, and give pupils opportunities to engage in active learning and finding things out for themselves.

Q 'What behaviour management strategies would you use?'

A Say that you would like to read the school's behaviour policy and, of course, that you realize you have to fit in with it. In addition, you think it would be good practice to discuss class rules with the class at the outset and have a set of rules to which everyone agrees, if that fits in with the school ethos. Explain that you would like to have a system of rewards and sanctions, and you believe a lot of misbehaviour can be avoided by making sure it is clear to pupils what is needed in terms of punctuality, and homework completed on time. Add that it is important that teachers speak politely and respectfully to pupils because sarcasm and cutting remarks provoke pupils into misbehaving.

Q 'How would you include the classroom assistants [CAs] in your planning?'

A Suggest that you could provide the CA with differentiated work and go through the lesson plan orally beforehand to make sure it was clear to him or her. Add that you realize it is important to know CAs' skills and try to give them tasks that give them the opportunity to make best use of their talents. Say that if you had a CA who was new, it would also be part of your task to train him or her to do the job.

Q 'All teachers are expected to contribute to extra-curricular activities. How do you see yourself contributing?'

A Describe what you can do — Duke of Edinburgh Award Scheme, Combined Cadet Force, amateur dramatics, or whatever. Add that you are willing to do so in the future but for the first term or two you would like to establish yourself and get the teaching load under control. (Never promise to start extra-curricular activities earlier, because it is just too much for an NQT — and once you have promised to do it, you cannot back out without creating a lot of ill feeling.)

Q 'Teamwork is important for the smooth running of the department. Why do you think you would be able to fit in well?'

A Agree wholeheartedly. Say how you worked in collaboration with others in other jobs you have had — unqualified teaching, working in a youth centre, working in an office, or other career before teaching. If appropriate, say you have met the rest of the team and liked them and are sure you could get on with them or would welcome the opportunity to do so.

Q 'If a pupil asked you a subject knowledge question and you did not know the answer, how would you respond?'

A Respond by explaining that you would not be afraid to say, 'I don't know. That's a good question. I'll definitely find out for you.' Of course, the response must be followed through by the next lesson.

Q 'How would you set about including pupils who spoke very little or no English in your lesson planning?'

A Say you would consult the EAL coordinator to find out more about their level of attainment, and get advice on how to differentiate the work for them. Also, talk to the EAL support teacher and plan the lesson with him or her. Give the EAL pupils a sheet with the keywords and meanings to keep on their desk as a reference. Use the list of suggestions in the 'Primary' section above.

Q 'If a pupil with a diagnosed learning difficulty was causing a habitual disturbance in the classroom, what would you do?'

A Say you would consult the special educational needs coordinator (SENCO) for help and advice. What you would do would of course depend on whether the pupil was able to help him- or herself. The pupil might need extra classroom support or it might be the case that the pupil was perfectly capable of behaving acceptably but was taking advantage of your being new. It would be wise to consult the parents, who are often able to give support.

Q 'If a parent telephones and demands dictatorially to see you immediately school is over, what do you do?'

A   Make clear that you would try not to show alarm. If you had another school commitment after lessons, you would say what it was – staff meeting, appointment with another parent, after-school club – and offer to see the parents after that. If they refused, you would offer 7.30 or 8 o'clock the following morning. If you had a personal appointment, such as a visit to the dentist, you would say that you could not see them but offer early the next morning. Tell the parent that if it is urgent, they could ask for an appointment with the head of department (HOD). Keep the HOD informed and ask him or her to be present when you meet an aggressive parent. You would try above all to let the parent realize that you were not prepared to be pushed around.

Q   'How would you deal with a pupil who almost never did his or her homework?'

A   Suggest that you would give the pupil a warning that they would have to stay in at lunch time (and follow through with the threat), or that you would phone the pupil's parents and ask them to ensure that the work was done. Again, you would have to carry through what you said. Ask whether your response fits in with the school policy.

Q   'How would you deal with a pupil who is consistently late?'

A   Give a warning that the time by which they are late will be made up by their being kept back in the classroom at break-time, and follow it through. Again ask about the school's policy.

Primary or secondary

Q   'What made you choose this school?'

A   This is a chance to pay them a compliment – for example, you like its ethos or friendly atmosphere, or you have heard favourable reports about the school from friends or parents. You have read the school's last Ofsted report or noticed that it was high on the league tables and you are impressed. Add that you want to work in a school where the pupils are conscientious and would find it stimulating to work in a school where standards are already high.

    Conversely, it is just as valid to say that you would find it stimulating to work in a school where the pupils present challenges. You could say that the post offers exactly the type of experience you most want, or that you want to develop a certain skill for which this post would give you an opportunity.

If you live close to the school, never say that its proximity is your first, second or even third reason. They are looking for teachers who are interested in the school, not their own convenience. However, you could add at the end that having no accommodation or travel problems would enable you to devote more time and energy to the job.

Q 'What skills and qualities can you bring to this school?'

A Have a list ready: boundless energy, ambition, eagerness to succeed in the profession, a strong interest in achieving progress, the experience of bringing up children, working with children in youth groups, and, if you live locally, an interest in or thorough knowledge of the neighbourhood and the community.

Q 'How would you deal with disruptive pupils?' (Beware of the school where you are asked this one, because it often means they have too many of them.)

A Say that first you would like to read the school's policy for dealing with it. Then you can add that it is important to find out the reasons for the behaviour before you can decide how to deal with it:

   ◆ It may be that the child is frustrated because he or she can never do the work and so you can suggest giving the child his or her own scheme of work. You might even have to give the child a few minutes of individual attention at the start of the lesson to ensure he or she can achieve something.

   ◆ If the child has a reading difficulty, it is important that he or she is assessed for dyslexia, because this condition can lead to great frustration and antisocial behaviour if left undiagnosed.

   ◆ The child may be a refugee or asylum seeker and be shell-shocked by suddenly having to cope in an unfamiliar culture. He or she may be literally shell-shocked, as some refugees have suffered appalling wartime hardships, in which case they may need counselling and a large helping of sympathy and encouragement.

   ◆ It may simply be that the child is spoilt rotten and cannot come to terms with not having his or her own way all the time, in which case you just have to clamp down and tell the child that if he or she wastes the class's valuable lesson time, you will waste the child's break-time (or equivalent) – and do carry out the threat.

◆   Also, you should talk to the parents in such a case. If you
    approach them tactfully, making it clear that you are most
    concerned about the child's progress, they may well be
    supportive.

Q   'Imagine that the inspector is coming and you have to present a
    model lesson and you want to impress. Describe what you would
    do.'
A   Describe a lesson in which there was much successful active
    learning.

Q   'Describe a scheme of lessons which you prepared and delivered
    when on teaching practice and which worked well.'
A   As the previous question. Have the answer prepared mentally.
    Explain your objectives, the activities and how you ensured that
    the less able were able to participate and the more able were
    extended.

Q   'How would you ensure inclusion?'
A   Ask them about the school's policy before you dive in. Say that it
    is important to differentiate the work so that pupils of lower ability
    can take part in lessons even if they cannot achieve as high a
    standard as the rest.
        Say you would use the support staff for pupils with special
    needs or pupils who may be in the early stages of learning English,
    because they are there to enable pupils to cope with areas of the
    curriculum where they might normally find it difficult to keep up
    with the rest of the class. Support teachers should also be involved
    in the planning of lessons, and you would encourage them to stay
    in the classroom and support the pupils while they have the same
    lesson as the rest of the class, even if their work is pitched at a
    lower level.
        If there is no support teacher available, where possible let
    children carry out practical work in mixed-ability groups because
    children do learn from each other.

Q   'Is there anything you would like to ask about the school?'
A   Always have something ready to ask so that it looks as though
    you have thought about it. You could ask any of these questions:
        ◆   'How will the staff here help me through the induction year?'
        ◆   'What are the school's main strengths?'

- ◆ 'What are the staff focusing on improving at the moment?'
- ◆ 'How supportive are the parents?'
- ◆ 'What percentage of children are on the special needs register/ EAL register?'

The closing question

Q 'If you were offered the post, would you accept it?' (This question means that they have not ruled you out.)

A Often, people do not make up their minds that they want a post until the interview. It is not unusual for applicants to change their minds during the interview.

If you want the post, then just say 'Yes'. At the end, shake hands, thank them for the interview and look happy.

Things to consider

You might want the post but want to negotiate on pay, in which case I should wait until the head telephones you to offer it, then say that you would love to accept the post as long as your other experience is recognized in the terms. If you are applying for a post in a shortage subject, you may well be in a strong position to negotiate.

If you have had teaching experience before your PGCE, you can reasonably ask them to acknowledge that in the salary point. If you have done the course as a mature student, having had a previous career, they are often willing to give you some credit for that. Always ask in a polite and respectful manner for your other experience to be considered. If you become aggressive or high-handed about it, you may deter the head from employing you and risk losing the job. If the terms are not what you want, then you will just have to decide between accepting it and trying to find a better-paid post.

If are offered a post but have applied for another post or are waiting for a reply from a previous interview, honesty is the best policy. Say that you want to hear from the other school before making a response and indicate when you expect to hear from that school. They may or may not allow you the time, but they will appreciate your honesty. It will count in your favour and show them that someone else is interested in you.

If you have said in the interview that you would take the post but then turn it down when offered it, there is a possibility that the head will pass on your name to other local heads as a teacher who does not do as they say they will do. Sometimes colleges are contacted and told that students have not stuck to their word.

Finally accepting a job

Accepting a job is a great relief because it enables you to study for your final exams or complete the final placement without stress – but beware, the job is conditional upon your passing your exams and school placements successfully.

Supply teaching in your school at the end of the summer term

Starting at a new school is always a steep learning curve for the first few weeks even if you are an experienced teacher, because each school is unique. The learning curve is even steeper if you are an NQT.

Heads normally invite NQTs to do some supply work in the school at the end of the summer term after their course is finished. If the head does not invite you to do so, I should ask whether it is possible. Even if the head says no, he or she will be pleased that you are keen. It is an opportunity to get to know the staff, the pupils, the geography and the general workings, and to ease yourself in gently.

If it is a wealthy school and you are very lucky, they may put you on the payroll throughout the summer holidays for working for part of June and July. At the very least, try to go to the school for a day or two before the end of the summer term.

When you start

NQTs are often excited and nervous at the same time. After all your hard work, you are actually on the threshold of your working life and about to be paid for it as well. These weeks are vitally important because you will be laying the foundation for your induction year, which of course you have to pass.

A few tips

Mind how you go:

◆   Dress as smartly as everyone else on the staff.
◆   Arrive at school at the same time as most of the staff.

Don't tread on toes:

◆   Some NQTs try to hide their nerves by acting smart. Teachers are never fooled by it and it rubs them up the wrong way.

◆ Keep any particularly strong views to yourself until you are established in the school. I have known new teachers to find themselves isolated after they have irritated everyone with their criticisms and suggestions for improvement.

◆ Don't get into disagreements with your colleagues on educational matters. Keep the path smooth.

◆ If you are being paid for the summer holidays as well as the days you work, don't advertise it to others. There may be a teacher who was not given the same privilege.

◆ Stay strictly out of school politics; it's more trouble than it's worth. However, keep your ears open. Knowing about underlying staff conflicts helps you to avoid getting involved in them.

Building relationships

◆ Chat to the support staff at breaks and get to know them.

◆ Be willing to learn from other teachers with experience. Don't be afraid to ask anything you don't know; they will be pleased you are eager to learn – but be aware how busy they are.

◆ Make sure you go to the staffroom at break-times. You'll be surprised how much more relaxed you will feel and how much better you will perform after a cup of tea and a snack, and it's always an opportunity to seek help if you need it, and to get to know your colleagues.

◆ If staff invite you to the pub after school, do go, even if you do not drink alcohol.

◆ Make friends with any other NQTs in the school because you will need each other's support in the busy year ahead.

◆ Try to establish a friendly rapport with your mentor (primary) or head of department (secondary) and be willing to defer to him or her.

◆ Remember that he or she can be a tower of strength to you and will be the one to assess your performance and decide whether you pass or fail your induction year.

◆ Stay on the right side of the head!

◆ Acknowledge to your colleagues that you are benefiting from their help. Make them feel it is worth your time being there and their time helping you.

Be proactive – show willingness:

◆ Offer to do playground duties.

◆ If you are asked to go into a class to observe how things are done, offer to be involved with the lesson.

In a primary school the head usually asks you to go into the classroom with the class that you will have the following year and their present teacher. This is a great chance to get to know them before you start. It also sets your mind at ease and stops you worrying for the summer. Try to find a chance to ask the teacher at least some of the following:

◆ what discipline strategies work well
◆ which children are most difficult to manage and what they respond to
◆ what support the children get for special needs and English as an additional language, if appropriate
◆ which parents are supportive, which are not and which are hostile
◆ which incentives work best

Sometimes the absentee rate among teachers increases at the end of the academic year, so the head might use you as a supply to cover their classes. This is often difficult as you can spend a fortnight being pushed from one end of the school to the other and having a different class every day. If, in a primary school, you are asked to teach an age group for which you are not trained, you may be tempted to try to get out of it, but it will enhance your credibility better if you don't. If you are nervous about it, try saying, 'I don't mind having a go, but you know I have no training for that age group. Is there someone who could show me what work they are doing and help me get something ready for them?'

This of course is another reason to be in early. If you are told at 7.45am what class you will have, you will be better prepared and feel more confident than if you have come rushing in at 8.45.

It won't matter too much if a day spent with an unfamiliar age group is not very successful, because they will be so pleased you were willing to try that it will not be held against you.

In a secondary school during this period, you may be asked to write some schemes of work or revamp old ones, or to cover classes for absent teachers. If you are asked to cover a class for a subject other than your own, there should be work left. If not, ask the relevant head of department for work.

During these weeks it is not so important to shine as a teacher. Your main aim is to become familiar with the school and its way of working and to get to know the staff and pupils – and, more importantly than you might imagine, to establish a positive working relationship with the head. If you achieve that, you will have laid a firm foundation for a very successful induction year and should pass with flying colours.

Supply teaching elsewhere

Sometimes heads do not want to employ you at the end of the term – or, more likely, they are unable to pay you. If this is the case, it is worthwhile to find some supply work anyway to get some quick experience and earn some extra money.

It is quite difficult to be a supply teacher at the end of the summer term because the pupils are tired and looking forward to the end of the year, so don't worry if it does not go as well as you hoped. It is always different in September.

There is a list of names and contact details of supply teaching agencies in Appendix 3 to help you find work.

Bibliography

Cowley, S. (2006), *Getting the Buggers to Behave*. London: Continuum International.

Fine, A. (1992), *The Chicken Gave It to Me*. London: Egmont.

Marryat, F. (1874), *The Children of the New Forest*. Whitefish, MT: Kessinger Publishing.

Shakespeare, W. (*c.* 1606), *King Lear*. Cambridge: Cambridge University Press.

Appendix 1
Abbreviations

A level	General Certificate of Education, Advanced level
ATL	Association of Teachers and Lecturers
BA	Bachelor of Arts
B.Ed.	Bachelor of Education
B.Sc.	Bachelor of Science
CA	classroom assistant
CV	curriculum vitae
DCSF	Department for Children, Schools and Families (formerly the DfES)
DfES	Department for Education and Skills
Dip. H.E.	Diploma in Higher Education
DT	design and technology
EAL	English as an Additional Language
EBITT	Employment Based Initial Teacher Training
EIS	Educational Institute of Scotland
EP	educational psychologist
EWO	educational welfare officer
GCSE	General Certificate of Secondary Education
GTP	Graduate Teacher Programme
GTTR	Graduate Teacher Training Registry
HM	Her Majesty's (government)
HND	Higher National Diploma
HOD	head of department
ICT	information and communication technology
IEP	individualized educational programme
INSET	in-service education of teachers
INTO	Irish National Teachers' Organisation
IWB	interactive whiteboard
LEA	local education authority
LSA	learning support assistant
NARIC	National Academic Recognition Information Centre

NASUWT	National Association of Schoolmasters and Union of Women Teachers
NC	National Curriculum
NQT	Newly Qualified Teacher
NUT	National Union of Teachers
Ofsted	Office for Standards in Education
PAT	Professional Association of Teachers
PE	physical education
PGCE	Postgraduate Certificate in Education
QCA	Qualifications and Curriculum Authority
QTS	Qualified Teacher Status
RE	religious education
RTP	Registered Teacher Programme
SAT	Standard Assessment Tasks
SCITT	School Centred Initial Teacher Training
SEN	special educational needs
SENCO	special educational needs coordinator
SLC	Student Loan Company
SSSS	Secondary Shortage Subject Scheme
TA	teaching assistant
TP	teaching practice
UCAS	Universities and Colleges Admissions Services
UTU	Ulster Teachers' Union

Appendix 2
Teachers' unions and associations: contact details

Association of School and College
  Leaders (ASCL)
(14,000 members)
130 Regent Road
Leicester LE1 7PG
Website: www.ascl.org.uk
Email: info@ascl.org.uk
Tel: 0116 299 1122
Fax: 0116 299 1123

Association of Teachers and
  Lecturers (ATL)
(160,000 members)
FREEPOST 7363
7 Northumberland Street
London WC2N 5RD
Website: www.atl.org.uk
Email: info@atl.org.uk
Tel: 020 7930 6441
Lo-Call: 0845 057 7000
Fax: 020 7930 1359

Educational Institute of Scotland
  (EIS)
(59,000 members)
46 Moray Place
Edinburgh EH3 6BH
Website: www.eis.org.uk
Email: enquiries@eis.org.uk
Tel: 0131 225 6244
Fax: 0131 220 3151

Irish National Teachers'
  Organisation (INTO)
(6,000 members)
23 College Gardens
Belfast BT9 6BS
Website: www.into.ie
Email: info@into.ie
Tel: 028 9038 1455
Fax: 028 90662803

Irish National Teachers'
  Organisation (INTO) in
  the Republic of Ireland
(30,000 members)
35 Parnell Square
Dublin 1
Website: www.into.ie
Email: info@into.ie
Tel: +353 1 8047700
Fax: +353 1 8722462
Lo-Call 1850 708708

National Association of
  Head Teachers
  (NAHT)
(28,000 members)
1 Heath Square
Boltro Road
Haywards Heath
West Sussex RH16 1BL

Email: membership@naht.org.uk
Tel: 01444 472470

National Association of
    Schoolmasters and Union of
    Women Teachers (NASUWT)
(234,000members)
FREEPOST BM 2337
Hillscourt Education Centre
Rose Hill
Rednal
Birmingham B45 8RS
Website: www.nasuwt.org.uk
Email: nasuwt@mail.nasuwt.org.uk;
    (membership)
    recruitment@mail.nasuwt.org.uk
Tel: 0121 453 6150; (membership)
    0121 457 6211
Fax: 0121 457 6208/6209

NASUWT in Scotland
6 Waterloo Place
Edinburgh EH1 3BG
Tel: 0131 523 1110
Fax: 0131 523 1119
Email: rc-
    scotland@mail.nasuwt.org.uk

NASUWT in Wales/NASUWT
    Cymru
Greenwood Close
Cardiff Gate Business Park
Cardiff CF23 8RD
Email: rc-wales-
    cymru@mail.nasuwt.org.uk
Tel: 029 2054 6080
Fax: 029 2054 6089

NASUWT in Northern Ireland
Ben Madigan House
Edgewater Office Park

Edgewater Road
Belfast BT3 9JQ
Email: rc-
    nireland@mail.nasuwt.org.uk
Tel: 028 9078 4480
Fax: 028 9078 4489

National Union of Teachers
    (NUT)
(300,000 members)
Hamilton House
Mabledon Place
London WC1H 9BD
Website: www.teachers.org.uk
Tel: 020 7388 6191; (membership
    hotline) 0845 300 1666
Fax: 020 7387 8458

Scottish Secondary Teachers'
    Association (SSTA)
(8,500 members)
West End House
14 West End Place
Edinburgh EH11 2ED
Website: www.ssta.org.uk
Email: info@ssta.org.uk
Tel: 0131 313 7300
Fax: 0131 346 8057

Ulster Teachers Union (UTU)
(7,000 members)
94 Malone Road
Belfast BT9 5HP
Website: www.utu.edu
Email: office@utu.edu
Tel: 028 9066 2216
Fax: 028 9068 3296

Universities and Colleges Union
(over 120,000 members)
Britannia Street

London WC1X 9JP
Website: www.ucu.org.uk
Email: hq@ucu.org.uk
Tel: 020 7837 3636
Fax: 020 7837 4403
Minicom: 020 7278 0470

Voice (formerly the Professional
   Association of Teachers)
(35,000 members)
2 St James' Court
Friar Gate
Derby DE1 1BT (for teachers in
   England and Wales)
Website:
   www.voicetheunion.org.uk

Email:
   enquiries@voicetheunion.
   org.uk
   membership@voicetheunion.
   org.uk
Tel: 01332 372 337
Fax: 01332 290 310

Voice in Scotland
13 Colme Street
Edinburgh EH3 6AA (for teachers
   in Scotland and Northern
   Ireland)
Email: scotland@pat.org.uk
Tel: 0131 220 8241
Fax: 0131 220 8350

Appendix 3
Teaching agencies and local council supply lists

Ambition 24 Hours Education
Website: www.ambition24hours
    education.co.uk
Email: info@supply-agency.co.uk
Tel: 0871 87 333 77

Capita Education Resourcing
Website: www.capitaers.co.uk
Email: enquiry.ers@capita.co.uk
Tel: 0800 731 6871 (primary)
Tel: 0800 731 6872 (secondary)
Tel: 0800 731 6873 (SEN and
    support staff)
Tel: 0800 316 1332 (further)
Branches nationwide

Career Teachers
Website:
    www.careerteachers.co.uk
Tel: 020 7382 4270
Email: info@careerteachers.co.uk

Class Act Teaching Services
Website: www.classact-
    teaching.co.uk
Email: info@classact-
    teaching.co.uk
Tel: 0800 028 6196; 01235 533
    358
Wiltshire, Oxfordshire,
    Warwickshire, Yorkshire

Conwy Council
Website: www.conwy.gov.uk
Email: information@conwy.co.uk
Tel: 01492 574000
Fax: 01492 592114

Cover Teachers
Website:
    www.coverteachers.co.uk
Email:
    enquiries@coverteachers.co.uk
Tel: 0117 973 5695
Fax: 0117 973 5045
South-West England

Eteach (England)
Website: www.eteach.com
Email: eteachagency@eteach.com
Tel: 0845 456 4384
Fax: 0870 236 2878

Eteach (Wales)
Email: ro@eteach.com
Tel: 02920 263 811

Hays Education
Website: www.hays.com/
    education/supply
Tel: 0800 716026
England and Wales
ITN Teachers

Email: admin@itnteachers.com
Tel: 020 7246 4777
London and Home Counties

Key Stage Teacher Supply
Website: www.keystage.co.uk
Tel: 01254 298616
Lancashire

Manchester Council
Website: www.manchester.gov.uk
Email:
city.council@manchester.go.uk
Tel: 0161 234 5000

Mark Education (Warrington)
Website:
www.markeducation.co.uk
Email: enquiries@itnmark.com
Tel: 01925 241 115
Fax: 01925 571 593

Mark Education (west London)
Email: west.london@itnmark.com
Tel: 0845 601 2165; 020 8326
1100
Fax: 020 8569 9532

Mark Education (London City)
Email: london.city@itnmark.com
Tel: 0845 230 2165; 020 7850
9100
Fax: 0870 130 1072; 020 7404
7883

Mark Education (Home Counties)
Email:
home.counties@itnmark.com
Tel: 0845 658 2165; 01223 370
042
Freefax: 0870 130 1072
Fax: 01223 370 053

Mark Education (Birmingham,
Coventry and Warwickshire)
Email: birmingham@itnmark.com
Freephone: 0800 169 4035
Tel: 0121 616 1666
Fax: 0121 616 2821

Mark Education (Bristol)
Email: bristol@itnmark.com
Freephone: 0800 169 4035
Tel: 0117 929 7999
Fax: 0117 930 4931

Mark Education (Leeds)
Email: leeds@itnmark.com
Freephone: 0800 169 4035
Tel: 0113 394 4243
Fax: 0113 394 4244

Mark Education (Leicester)
Email: leicester@itnmark.com
Freephone: 0800 169 4035
Tel: 0116 242 4162
Fax: 0116 242 4163

Mark Education (Newcastle)
Email: newcastle@itnmark.com
Freephone: 0800 169 4035
Tel: 0191 260 2578
Fax: 0191 260 2579

Mark Education (Northampton)
Email: northampton@itnmark.com
Tel: 01604 622 133
Fax: 0116 242 4163

Mark Education (Preston)
Email: preston@itnmark.com
Freephone: 0800 169 4035
Tel: 01772 880 741
Fax: 01772 880 523

Mark Education (Southampton)
Email:
southampton@itnmark.com
Freephone: 0800 169 4035
Tel: 02380 635 800
Fax: 02380 635 696

Mark Education (Warrington,
Manchester and Liverpool)
Email: warrington@itnmark.com
Freephone: 0800 169 4035
Tel: 01925 242 002
Fax: 01925 242 029

Mark Education (Wolverhampton)
Email:
wolverhampton@itnmark.com
Freephone: 0800 169 4035
Tel: 01902 810 011
Fax: 01902 810 012

Masterlock Recruitment (London)
Website: www.masterlock.co.uk
Email: info@masterlock.co.uk
Tel: 020 7229 6699
Fax: 020 7938 4977

Masterlock Recruitment (West
Country)
Email: bristol@masterlock.co.uk
Tel: 0117 915 4567
Fax: 0117 925 4570

Protocol Teachers
Website: www.protocol-
teachers.com
Email: info@protocol-
teachers.com
Tel: 020 7440 8449; 0845 450
9450
Branches nationwide

Quay Education Services (Milton
Keynes)
Website:
www.quayeducation.co.uk
Email:
success@quayeducation.co.uk
Tel: 01908 663 039
Fax: 01908 238 288

Quay Education Services
(Hammersmith office)
Email:
educate@quayeducation.co.uk
Tel: 0208 563 8885
Fax: 0208 563 8599

Quay Education Services
(Sheffield office)
Email:
learn@quayeducation.co.uk
Tel: 0114 273 1616
Fax: 0114 273 0606

Quay Education Services
(Liverpool office)
Email:
progress@quayeducation.co.uk
Tel: 0151 709 0400
Fax: 0151 709 1888

Quay Education Services (Leeds
office)
Email:
develop@quayeducation.co.uk
Tel: 0113 391 2804
Fax: 0113 246 1939

Quay Education Services
(Warrington office)
Email: study@quayeducation.co.uk
Tel: 0845 895 0305
Fax: 0845 355 1187

Quay Education Services
(Wolverhampton office)
Email:
achieve@quayeducation.co.uk
Tel: 01902 710 723
Fax: 01902 427 111

Renaissance Education
Website: www.edulon.co.uk
Email: teach@edulon.co.uk
Tel: 020 7385 9768; (24 hours)
020 7953 4053
Fax: 020 7953 4054
Greater London

Select Education
Website:
www.selecteducation.co.uk
Email: education@
selecteducation.com
Tel: 01582 406800
Fax: 01582 406815
Branches nationwide

Standby Teachers
Website:
www.standbyteachers.com
Tel: 01943 86461
Yorkshire

Supply Desk
Website:
www.thesupplydesk.co.uk
Email: info@thesupplydesk.co.uk

Tel: 0114 2834900
Fax: 0114 2834908

Teachers UK
Website: www.teachers-uk.co.uk
Tel: 0800 068 1117
London and Home Counties

Teaching Supply Agency
Website: www.teaching-
agency.co.uk
Tel: 01344 482708
Fax: 01344 482921

Timeplan
Website: www.timeplan.com
Email: jen.taaffe@timeplan.net
Tel: 020 8371 8000
Fax: 020 8371 8031
See website for local offices
England and Scotland

Trust Education
Website:
www.trusteducation.co.uk
Tel: 020 7328 0000
London

West Country Educational
Agency
Website: www.westcountry
agency.co.uk
Email: staff@westcountry.co.uk
Tel: 01225 706726
Fax: 01225 706698

Appendix 4
Subject associations

Association for Advice and
Support in Art and Design
Website: www.afour.org.uk

National Association of Music
Educators (NAME)
Website: www.name.org.uk

National Dance Teachers
Association
Website: www.nadt.org.uk

National Society for Education in
Art and Design
Website: www.nsead.org

Economics and Business
Education Association
Website: www.ebea.org.uk

Association for Citizenship
Teaching
Website: www.teachingcitizen
ship.org.uk

Design and Technology
Association
Website: www.data.org.uk

National Association of Advisers
and Inspectors in Design and
Technology

Website: www.naaidt.org.uk

English Association
Website: www.le.ac.uk/engassoc

English and Media Centre
Website:
www.englishandmedia.co.uk

Media Education Association
Website: www.mediaed
association.org.uk

National Association for the
Teaching of English
Website: www.nate.org.uk

National Drama
Website:
www.nationaldrama.co.uk

United Kingdom Literacy
Association (UKLA)
Website: www.ukla.org

Geographical Association
Website: www.geography.org.uk

Royal Geographical Society with
Institute of British
Geographers
Website: www.rgs.org

Historical Association
Website: www.history.org.uk

Schools History Project
Website: www.leedstrinity.ac.uk/
shp

Naace (Association for ICT)
www.naace.org.uk

Association for Language
Learning
Website: www.all-
languages.org.uk

National Centre for Languages
Website: www.cilt.org.uk

Association of Teachers of
Mathematics
Website: www.atm.org.uk

Advisory Committee on
Mathematics Education
(ACME)
Website: www.acme-uk.org

Joint Mathematical Council of the
United Kingdom
Website: www.jmcuk.org.uk

Mathematical Association
Website: www.m-a.org.uk

Association for Physical
Education (afPE)
Website: www.afpe.org.uk

PSHE Subject Association
Website: www.pshe-
association.org.uk

Religious Education Council of
England and Wales
Website: www.religious
educationcouncil.org

Association for Science Education
Website: www.ase.org.uk

British Association for the
Advancement of Science
Website: www.the-ba.net

Engineering and Technology
Board
Website: www.etechb.co.uk

Institute of Biology
Website: www.iob.org

Institute of Physics
www.iop.org

Royal Society for Chemistry
(RSC)
Website: www.rsc.org/Education/
Teachers/index.asp

Appendix 5
Suggested further reading

Bennett, H. (2005), *The Ultimate Teachers' Handbook*. London: Continuum International.

Bowden, D., Gray, B. and Thody, A. (2000), *The Teachers' Survival Guide*. London: Continuum International.

Bubb, S. (2003), *The Insiders' Guide for New Teachers*. London: Kogan Page.

Cowley, S. (2003), *Guerilla Guide to Teaching*, 2nd ed. London: Continuum International.

Cowley, S. (2003), *How to Survive the First Year of Teaching*. London: Continuum International.

Index